COMING CLEAN

COMING CLEAN

THE STUDY GUIDE TO KICKING HABITS

THOMAS G. BANDY

250.973

ABINGDON PRESS / Nashville

COMING CLEAN: THE STUDY GUIDE TO *KICKING HABITS*

Copyright © 2001 by Abingdon Press

This book is printed on recycled, acid-free paper.

Library of Congress Cataloging-in-Publication Data

Bandy, Thomas G., 1950-
  Coming clean : the study guide to Kicking habits / Thomas G. Bandy.
    p. cm.
  ISBN 0-687-05024-3 (alk. paper)
    1. Church renewal. I. Title.

BV600.3 .B355 2001
250'.973—dc21

2001022271

Scripture quotations, unless otherwise indicated, are from the *New Revised Standard Version of the Bible,* copyright © 1989, by the Division of Christian Education of the National Council of the Churches of Christ in the United States of America. Used by permission. All rights reserved.

01 02 03 04 05 06 07 08 09 10—10 9 8 7 6 5 4 3 2 1

MANUFACTURED IN THE UNITED STATES OF AMERICA

This book is dedicated to all those Christian leaders
whose callings have been renewed,
whose careers have been reoriented,
and whose hopes for God's Realm have been revived,
because of the thriving church system.

Seize the moment,
go with the flow,
and never look back.

CONTENTS

How to Use This Study Guide 9

The Story of Bob and Sally 13

PART ONE

Is There Hope for Your Congregation? 23

Session 1: What Does It Mean to Be Addicted? 25
Session 2: Why Do People Yearn for God? 35

PART TWO

A Better Way to Be the Church! 39

Session 1: Do You Want to Change People or Enroll
   Newcomers? 42
Session 2: Do You Want to Grow Disciples or Inform
   Members? 46
Session 3: Do You Want to Fulfill Lives or
   Fill Offices? 50
Session 4: Do You Want to Equip Ministers or
   Supervise Committees? 53
Session 5: Do You Want to Deploy Servants or Keep
   Everybody Happy? 57

PART THREE

Escaping the Tornado of Church Decline! **61**

    Session 1: The Energy Field **66**
    Session 2: The Circle of Life **71**
    Session 3: The Stability Triangle **75**
    Session 4: The Core of Spirituality **80**

PART FOUR

Transforming the Congregation! **85**

    Session 1: Build a Team Vision **92**
    Session 2: Motivate Spiritual Growth **102**
    Session 3: Free Leaders to Lead **113**
    Session 4: Streamline the Organization **122**
    Session 5: Birth a New System **134**
    What Do We Do Now? **144**

Leading Change
    A Bible Study for Those Who Want to Be Transformational
Leaders **147**

Index **153**

HOW TO USE THIS STUDY GUIDE

Welcome! If you are now reading *Kicking Habits: Welcome Relief of Addicted Churches,* then you are in the process of reading a book that has literally changed lives. This book has become so significant that it is now being released in a new, revised edition. This study guide is keyed to the revised edition.

This means that *Kicking Habits* is also a book that will increase your sense of personal and congregational stress. In the years after this book was first published, it has been praised by turn-around church leaders as the most formative book in their long-range planning—and it has literally been burned by angry church members. This book has gotten some clergy hired and some clergy fired. It has motivated some laity to heroic action, and other laity to quit the church.

Many congregations have responded to this book positively by breaking through barriers that have beset them for years, deepening spirituality, multiplying ministries, and expanding missions locally and globally. Some congregations have seen the path to a thriving church, and decided that they would rather die. There is a price to pay if you want your church to grow. This *Coming Clean: A Study Guide to Kicking Habits* will help you decide if you are ready to pay that price.

This study guide may be a little different from the ones you have used before. It does not exactly follow *Kicking Habits* chapter by chapter. Instead, it helps you feel the whole flow of congregational life. It assumes that you will not just be reading a chapter at a time, but studying the whole book at once. The guide also assumes that you will not be studying the book as an individual, but that you will be studying it with a group of at least three people and no more than about twenty-one people.

Here are some suggestions about the group experience:

1. Every participant in the group should read *Kicking Habits* completely *before* the study begins. The page references in *Coming Clean* link the reader to the upgrade edition of *Kicking Habits*.
2. Plan to meet on a regular basis, in an informal setting, *away from the church building itself*. Meet in a home for some sessions, and deliberately meet in any public place for other sessions. A restaurant, a shopping mall food court, or a sports arena can be good choices. Do not worry if meeting in these public places is noisy or distracting. That's exactly why you are there. God is speaking to you from the culture around you, not just this book.
3. However large your group may be, organize yourselves in *triads*. Experience this process as a triad. Sit together in the study group as a triad. Respond to the questions and do the exercises as a triad. In between sessions, communicate within the triad about your questions, doubts, discoveries, and anxieties. Most important, every triad should covenant together to pray daily for the mission of Christ through your congregation, and for the current study to bear fruit for positive change. Triad members should hold each other accountable for their shared discipline of prayer.
4. Begin each study session in quiet meditation. *Do not speak aloud.* At the beginning of every session, you will find a suggested object to place at the center of your gathering. Let that object focus the participants on the study theme. For those sessions held in a private home, *always* listen to music during the meditation time, *but make sure it is a different radio station every time*.
5. Let the process find its own pace. If you do not complete a section of the guide in the time provided, return to it again in the next session. It is important that everyone has an opportunity to speak his or her mind. Therefore, encourage the talkative to be patient, and encourage the shy to speak.
6. Be free to customize the process. Adjust each session for the unique needs of the participants. Be sensitive to difficulties in hearing or speech, other languages that may be primary for participants, and images or metaphors that speak clearly and powerfully to other cultures.
7. End each study session in prayer. *Pray aloud.* Pray especially for

each member of the group by name, and for the Holy Spirit to use the group to be a blessing for the whole congregation.

This study guide assumes that members of the group are not only learning together, but that they are joining in a shared spiritual discipline. Therefore, strongly encourage participants to commit themselves to faithful attendance for the duration of the study. If newcomers join after the third meeting, the group should quickly recap previous key discoveries and insights.

Here are some suggestions about group leadership:

1. Almost all groups work best with a designated leader or team of leaders. Avoid rotating leadership in the group.
2. Clergy should only lead a group if a layperson is teamed with him or her.
3. Group leaders should prepare for each session in advance of the gathering, and feel free to customize the process as necessary. For sessions held in private homes, leaders should pay special attention to the meditation focus and music background. A meditation object is suggested for each session. The music should match the variety offered in community radio stations. For sessions held in public places, leaders should make advance reservations or arrangements if needed. Strive to find places where heat or air conditioning is comfortable, and away from cigarette smoke.
4. Be very intentional about organizing and encouraging triads. Ask for feedback from triads based on their conversations between sessions. Ask if triads have been diligent in their prayers for the church and the process. (Note: If the group leadership is a team, leaders should be in different triads.)
5. Reading *Kicking Habits* increases stress. Therefore, anticipate the emergence of strong positive and negative feelings. People *do not* have to agree with one another as each session concludes. Work for mutual respect, not harmony. Build relationships around shared spirituality, rather than a common point of view.
6. Communicate regularly with the pastor or the worship planning team or both. They may want to share discoveries or ideas in the context of congregational preaching and worship.

11

The goal of this study is to deepen the self-awareness of the congregation, and sharpen its sensitivity to God's call to be with Jesus in mission. The goal is *not* to complete a strategic plan for the church, or to present policy or program recommendations to the board. You will know that you have succeeded in the study group if individuals have greater clarity and enthusiasm about what it means to thrive as a church in the twenty-first century.

Finally, this study guide is intentionally linked to other books written by myself and my partner Bill Easum. You will find references to chapters and sections of other books all through the study guide, which will help you pursue particular topics of leadership, worship, and organization in even greater depth.

The thriving church model itself is studied in part 2 with explicit reference to *Facing Reality: A Congregational Mission Assessment Tool*. This is a consultation tool and workbook designed to complement *Kicking Habits*, which helps congregational leaders explore in depth all eleven subsystems of congregational life. Throughout this study guide you will find references to, and connections with, *Facing Reality*. Not only will the study guide help you apply the insights of *Kicking Habits* to your congregation, it will provide a helpful bridge for those who plan to use *Facing Reality* to thoroughly research their congregational life and mission to discern strengths, weaknesses, and hidden patterns of corporate addiction. *Facing Reality: A Congregational Mission Assessment Tool*, and all other books mentioned, are available from Abingdon Press, or through *Easum, Bandy & Associates* (*www.easumbandy.com*).

Finally, you will find additional opportunities to be in personal dialogue with me, or with my colleagues in *Easum, Bandy & Associates* simply by using our website. Look for ongoing Internet forums, face-to-face summits, and other opportunities for consultation by joining the *EBA* community.

THE STORY OF BOB AND SALLY

In *Kicking Habits*, the story of Bob and Sally is divided among the chapters. Here it is again as single narrative. Read it once more in preparation for further study.

Allow me to introduce you to "Bob and Sally Public." Their real names may be Boris, Juan, Said, Hung, or Takemura, and Mariska, Maria, Linh, or Zarpana. They may belong to any number of North American subcultures or "publics." They may be married, divorced, divorced for the third time, single, living together, parenting their own children, or parenting children from their present partner's past partnerships. They may be any age, at any economic level, and have any educational background. Whoever they may be, they share five things in common:

1. Bob and Sally are simultaneously bored and frantic.
2. Bob and Sally wrestle with low self-esteem and broken relationships.
3. Bob and Sally wish they had a better life without knowing what it would be.
4. Bob and Sally usually do not leave home Sunday mornings unless it is to play softball or buy the morning paper.
5. Bob and Sally live next door to you.

Bob and Sally represent the fastest-growing segment of the North American population. They are the "Gentiles" of the new millennium. They are the spiritually yearning, institutionally alienated public.

13

Bob and Sally have changed forever the meaning of that simple phrase "going to church." It used to mean an intention to attend worship an hour a week, and a commitment to support a charitable institution. In the new millennium, it means a yearning to experience God through the week, and a covenant to be involved in Christian mission.

Bob and Sally probably cannot accurately describe in advance what they are seeking in a church. They may only be "church shopping," and their "shopping list" may well not reflect the spiritual foods that in the end will truly satisfy and fulfill. Their list may include:

"center aisle sanctuary"
"good nursery"
"low financial expectations"
"friendly people"
"nice minister"

but in the end they may well gain all of these *and still drop out of the church.* It is the system of church life that will be crucial to Bob and Sally. It is the whole flow of spiritual experience that will be vital. It is the coherence and value of the whole movement from seeker to servant, and from healing to healer, that will hold them in the life of the church. Their initial shopping list will fade into secondary importance. What will determine their future participation is whether or not the church has helped them go deeper, soar higher, see farther, reach wider, and live better one day at a time.

FRUSTRATED CHURCH SHOPPING

Bob and Sally Public have come to St. Friendly-on-the-Hill Church with their young family. A lay greeter welcomes them as they enter the narthex, and provides them with directions to the coatracks and washrooms. The greeter also gives them "Newcomer Name tags" and introduces them to other members of the church, and eventually, to the minister.

"Reverend," Sally says, "we're new in the neighborhood, and we would like to make friends in the community. We also want our

14

kids to start learning Christian values in your Sunday school—and, oh yes!—our new baby has not been baptized."

"Fine, fine," replies the Reverend Enabler. "Here's a booklet about our church and denomination. There just happens to be a Baptism Class beginning this week for six sessions, so we can discuss it. Now let's introduce the kids to their Sunday school teacher, and then grab some coffee."

In due course, the kids are enrolled, the baby is baptized, and Bob and Sally become recognizable figures during coffee hour. Soon people know them by their first names. Before long speculation begins as to Sally's suitability for nursery care leadership, and Bob's potential for the Property Committee. (It turns out he is an electrician! Hooray!)

A year later Bob and Sally have "gone missing." It happened slowly. First they only appeared in worship every other week—then the kids began appearing in Sunday school every other week. Then less. Elders visitation reported how busy a dual career couple could be, and how hard it was to attend regularly with young children. They appeared again at Christmas—then the pledge was discovered to be in arrears.

"No, no," said Sally on the telephone with the church secretary. "There's no problem. We really love you folks. You're so friendly. Everything's fine—we're just so busy!" And yet, a year later, Bob and Sally have vanished into the spiritual fog.

DID THEY FIND A GOOD CHURCH—OR DID A GOOD CHURCH FIND THEM?

Bob and Sally Public have come to New Hope-in-the-Heart Church with their young family. "A lay greeter welcomes them as they enter the foyer, and personally introduces them to the trained nursery staff who will care for their toddler, and the trained children's ministers who will lead the Sunday school. The security system to keep the children safe is briefly explained. Bob and Sally are then led back to the foyer where they already hear loud, rhythmic music and singing. "Just go on in and sit where you like!" says the greeter. "It's great to meet you!"

As Bob and Sally walk toward the worship center, they see all around them visual displays of missions, adult faith development

15

opportunities, and spirituality groups that are available. The worship experience is fast-paced, dramatic, visual, and requires no printed helps. The message-sharer seems to be speaking directly to them. Trained lay counselors around the room occasionally interact with participants with a laugh, a hug, or a conversation. And the music never stops. Bob and Sally feel glad they are here.

During refreshment time, one of the lay counselors talks with them. "We used to go to St. Friendly-on-the-Hill Church," says Sally with some embarrassment. "The truth is, we lied to them . . . or maybe we lied to ourselves. Anyway, we told them we wanted to make friends, but the truth is we already have a great bunch of friends in the softball league." Here Sally takes a deep breath. "And we told the minister that we wanted our baby baptized, but the truth is I WANTED TO BE DIFFERENT."

A year later Bob and Sally still do not know everyone by first name, but they attend a small, intimate, spirituality and faith development group every week in a participant's home. Neither Sally nor Bob belong to any committee, and rarely attend church meetings, but each is passionately involved in a mission. People who know them say they have changed. They never miss a worship service, even during the summer.

DARE TO COMPARE!

Occasionally with friends, Bob and Sally Public reflect on their very different experiences with St. Friendly-on-the-Hill Church and New Hope-in-the-Heart Church. They are not quite sure why these two churches are so different. Many specific things come to mind. St. Friendly's uses a long printed bulletin in worship, does everything through meetings, recruits as many people as possible into offices, and is always worried about money. New Hope prints newsletters and produces videos, does everything through small spirituality cell groups, encourages people to discern their spiritual gifts, and is always thinking about new ministries.

Bob and Sally are aware, however, that these specific contrasts do not explain the core of the difference. There is simply a different "spirit" about the two churches.

Bob and Sally remember vividly two parallel conversations they had with the pastoral leaders of these churches. Some years ago, St. Friendly-on-the-Hill Church received a new ordained minister. Bob and Sally asked him one day if he had found it difficult to enter into the life of a new church. His response was as follows:

"No, Bob," he said. "It's true that St. Friendly's is unique in many ways. The sanctuary is more beautiful than many in which I have led worship, and the organ is the best I've ever heard. And it's true that there is a harmony here that many churches have yet to achieve. I'm glad I came here. The fact is, however, that every church I have served is basically the same. They all seem to have the same group of unusual personalities. They all have trouble keeping the youth involved. An annual deficit is always a burden, and the basic categories of church programs look pretty much alike. Walk into any church of our denomination, and you will feel at home. I guess it's part of our church 'ethos'."

In contrast to this conversation, Bob and Sally remembered talking to the pastoral leader of New Hope-in-the-Heart Church. He was sharing his experience of his first years with the congregation.

"Sally," he said, "it was tough. Within weeks I realized that New Hope-in-the Heart Church was unlike anything I had experienced in past congregations. It wasn't just that people had different names for programs, or that the sanctuary didn't have a pulpit. People just behaved in ways I didn't expect. Routine things I used to do, that were quite effective, didn't work here. On the other hand, some things I did by chance, or by simple intuition, seemed to succeed beyond expectation. The truth is that my seminary never equipped me for **this** kind of church, and I had a lot of learning to do. When my colleagues visit here, they know it's a whole new 'ball game'!"

Call it a "new ball game." Call it a "different spirit." Call it a return to "first-century" church experience. Bob and Sally have trouble putting their finger on the essential difference. They just know it is a different **system** of church life.

INSIDE NEW HOPE

Bob and Sally Public have been involved in New Hope-in-the-Heart Church for long enough to know that it is different from most other churches they know in the area. The Protestant evan-

17

gelical churches are perplexed that New Hope-in-the-Heart Church celebrates transforming personal experiences with God, and yet does not impose an extensive doctrinal agenda with which people must agree. The folks at New Hope-in-the-Heart Church seem to have an unsettling freedom to discover and define their faith for themselves. The Protestant "mainstream" churches are perplexed that New Hope-in-the-Heart Church releases so much energy into the community for social reform and charitable outreach, and yet as a body takes relatively few public ideological stands.

One day Bob and Sally happen to be with a group from the local community "ministry association," which is trying to build mutual understanding among the religious groups of the area. People are asked to draw a picture of how their churches operate.

Most people draw structural diagrams with solid or dotted straight lines, and large or small boxes. All of the committees, groups, and offices are depicted; many lines of accountability and communication are clearly defined. It looks very efficient. It does not seem to work. Everyone is doing "restructuring." Bob and Sally Public overhear the tales of woe:

"We tried inverting the triangle," says one church, "so that real authority in the church lies with a consensus of the people, rather than with the minister and a few board members."

"We've been amalgamating committees," says another church, "since we can't find enough people to serve them anyway."

"But we've been multiplying committees," replies a third church. "We want to get as many people involved in decision making as possible."

"We took a whole year to rewrite our mission statement, and another year to rewrite our church constitution," says a fourth church. "We've decreased the number of years anyone can serve in office, and added congregational meetings in the year."

"We tried that," says a fifth church. "We rewrote out mission statement and constitution to build more continuity with the past. Our officers now serve more years, and the congregation only meets every other year."

On and on, the restructuring discussion continues. It becomes apparent to Bob and Sally that nothing seems to work. No matter how they deal the cards, the game is always the same. Despite all the structural tinkering, and the years of writing new mission statements and constitutions, nothing has really changed.

Finally, Bob and Sally are asked to describe how their church works. Given the context of the conversation, this isn't easy. Where others draw straight lines, Bob and Sally only seem to draw curved lines. Where others draw boxes, they draw circles. Where others have a diagram in which everything is linked to everything else at least twice, Bob and Sally have a diagram in which some things don't seem to be linked to anything at all! The other diagrams all look so neat, tidy, and complete. Bob's and Sally's diagram looks messy, untidy, and incomplete. Reactions from both "evangelical" and "mainline" church partners are unanimous.

"This looks like anarchy!" some say. "This is chaos! People are allowed to go all over the place. Where is the accountability? How can you make sure nobody does something stupid or down-right immoral?"

"This looks like dictatorship!" others say. "The ordained minister and a few lay leaders will control everything. How can you make sure that your leadership will not do something stupid or immoral?"

"Where is the group identity?" still others protest. "The diversity is so great that there is nothing—no clear convictions, no firm Christian stand on the issues—to hold people together with a common cause!"

Bob and Sally do their best to explain. It is not anarchy, but there is an incredible ferment of activity. It is not dictatorship, but the leaders of the church are powerful motivators and visionaries. The people are, indeed, incredibly diverse, but the fact that they all agree about almost nothing doesn't matter.

Although Bob and Sally are not very good at explaining it, especially with the terminology and conceptual framework assumed by the local ministry association, they do have one telling argument. "It works." Somehow New Hope-in-the-Heart Church avoids anarchy and dictatorship, does not seem to do anything overwhelmingly stupid or immoral, and manages to celebrate amazing harmony among many really different people. Perhaps to understand how this is possible, the ministry association will have to step beyond its conceptual assumptions—or simply confront some of its addictions!

FROM HERE TO THERE

Bob and Sally Public are now joyously involved in New Hope-in-the Heart Church. They have been changed, gifted, called, equipped, and sent. Even now they continue to feel the transforming touch of God in their lives, and they continue to discover new dimensions to the gifts they been given. Their own sense of calling has led them to appreciate the many diverse callings of people around them, and they value more than ever the great basic vision of the church which allows all these missions to happen in the Body of Christ. The fact that they have a sense of their own destiny, that the church has invested itself to train them, and that the church has trusted them to do ministry, fills them with a deep sense of worth and responsibility.

Yet Bob and Sally have not forgotten St. Friendly-on-the-Hill Church. After all, they really were friendly, good people. True, some people feel rejected and mad that Bob and Sally left the church. A few others can't get over their sense of guilt that somehow they failed Bob and Sally. And a few more still think Bob and Sally left because the nursery wasn't carpeted, or because the hymnbook wasn't good enough, and they are still tinkering with the program in the belief that Bob and Sally can be lured back again. Most of the people, however, remain very friendly with Bob and Sally, and marvel at the change in their lives. Some of their teens are involved in Bob's drug addiction ministry; and some of their members have talked to Sally about her dream of an elder day-care center. The model railroad youth ministry, of course, has been described in the local newspaper.

Some of the St. Friendly-on-the-Hill people begin to talk with Bob and Sally more seriously. They actually came to visit as representatives of the church, seeking only to listen and learn from Bob and Sally. Others are actually surveying complete strangers in the community to discover what they can do to address public interest more effectively. Bob and Sally are deeply moved. Perhaps New Hope-in-the-Heart Church can help St. Friendly-

on-the-Hill, not simply to imitate their church life but to discover some new way of thriving that is right for the unique context of St. Friendly-on-the-Hill.

Bob and Sally talk about it with the woman who has been their mentor, small group leader, and spiritual guide throughout their church experience. This is the woman who first visited them as newcomers to the church, who sat with them in worship, and who guided them into the small group spirituality of the church. Edith tells them a remarkable story:

"You know," Edith says, "New Hope-in-the-Heart Church was not always this way. In fact, some years ago, it was a traditional, declining church just like St. Friendly. The congregation at the time was called "Old Faithful Church." Back in the forties and fifties it was a really big church, but by the eighties only about thirty people worshiped inside the big, old, beautiful building. Basically, they were great folks, who were in deep trouble. Then one day things began to change—really change. Funny to say, when things began to change, almost everyone between fifty and sixty years of age left the church. It seemed like the only remaining ones were either under forty, or over ninety! But I guess they figured they didn't have anything to lose, so they kept on changing. Eventually they tore down the old building, relocated, and things started happening in a brand new way. Looking back on it, I think even they thought it was a bit crazy. Now, I guess, it looks like the power of God."

I

IS THERE HOPE FOR YOUR CONGREGATION?

Read the preface and chapters 1 and 12 of
Kicking Habits (pages 11-19, 27-41, and 237-58)

Yes! There is hope for your congregation! There are examples of "turn-around" congregations in every denomination in North America. These congregations may be urban, suburban, or rural. Some of these congregations were literally on the brink of bankruptcy and near closure. Some had been stuck on a plateau of mission for over a century. Some had been burdened by conflict that never seemed to end. Some were quite happy and harmonious, but never seemed to bear any fruit for mission. There is hope for your congregation—*but you will have to change!*

The changes that must occur are not just program adjustments, staff additions, or property renovations. It is *change* for your whole way of life as a congregation. It is exciting and scary at the same time.

Before you launch into the next two sessions, take time to read and discuss the following scripture passage, and complete the following exercise. Stand back and survey your life experience so far. What do you really hope for in the future? Really? No holding back, no limitations, no reservations. Go wild, dream impossible dreams, see visions. In your deepest heart, what is your hope?

Bible
Study   Read *and memorize* the following scripture verses:

> Joel 2:28 I will pour out my spirit on all flesh;
> your sons and your daughters shall prophesy,
> your old men shall dream dreams,
> and your young men shall see visions.

Isaiah 41:10   Do not fear, for I am with you,
                do not be afraid, for I am your God;
                I will strengthen you, I will help you,
                I will uphold you with my victorious right hand.

Isaiah 61:1   The spirit of the Lord GOD is upon me,
                because the LORD has anointed me;
                he has sent me to bring good news to the
                    oppressed,
                to bind up the brokenhearted,
                to proclaim liberty to the captives,
                and release to the prisoners.

Luke 4:20-21   The eyes of all in the synagogue were fixed on
                [Jesus]. Then he began to say to them, "Today this
                scripture has been fulfilled in your hearing."

Recite these scriptures aloud constantly, to yourself and to others in your study group, so long as you meet together.

Exercise Share with one another your deepest yearnings for yourself, your loved ones, and the world.

If your hopes were realized, how would people behave?

If your hopes were realized, what would the church look like?

If your hopes were realized, how would your life be different?

Session 1
What Does It Mean to Be Addicted?

Goal   In this session we will understand how the metaphor of addiction applies to our congregational life, and begin to uncover your stress about change.

Prayer Focus   Use a perpetual motion toy made of a series of steel balls, suspended in a row from a bar. As one outside ball strikes the row, its energy kicks out the ball at the other side, which then swings back again to strike the row and kick the other outside ball outward. Start the balls now. Watch them go back and forth. Click, click, click, click. As the balls swing, read each of the following statements with a few seconds of silence. Think about your church.

Everything is interrelated. Little things affect the whole.
Actions and reactions are so predictable. Add or take away a ball, but nothing changes.
The more you experience it, the more annoying the experience becomes.
Eventually, the machine begins to wear down, and stop.
Once stopped, the quiet is oddly uncomfortable. You long to start it up again!

Bible Study   Read aloud the story of the healing of Legion found in Mark 5:1-20.

People today experience addictions like people long ago experience demon possession. They cannot control their lives. They are driven to destroy their own

25

lives. They cannot escape the power of evil. Eventually they are both accepted and trapped in the larger context of a sick society. Discuss these questions:

Why does Legion live like he does?

How many addictions can a person have?

What does it mean to experience the intervention of a Higher Power?

Why do the neighbors beg Jesus to leave?

Now read the story aloud once more. However, when you come to Jesus' words in verse 19, shout the words together in unison: *"Go home to your friends, and tell them how much the Lord has done for you, and what mercy he has shown you."*

Discussion

An addiction is a self-destructive behavior pattern that is habitually repeated, and yet chronically denied. It is a way of life that seems so natural that we do not even think about it. It is a pattern of living that seems inevitable. It is the predictable way we react to things. It is how we behave whenever we are in a state of confusion, uncertainty, conflict, or stress. *There we go again!*

Every human being is addicted to something, and many things. It is another way of describing our sinfulness. Sometimes we make "new year's resolutions" to change our behavior, and fail. At other times we recite confessions in worship services but never feel quite cleansed or reassured.

What are some of the things to which people are addicted?

What are some of the ways that you personally are addicted?

What are some of the self-destructive behavior patterns you have seen over the years at church?

Exercise

In the upgrade version of *Kicking Habits* (pages 19-24) and in *Facing Reality: A Congregational Mission Assessment Tool* (pages 94-97) you will find a new extended version of "The Church Stress Test." Each statement may feel like a "bombshell," and they are designed to unsettle and disturb. Think of the test as a geological exploration technique. Geologists explode dynamite charges underground and then measure the seismic reaction in order to map the hidden layers of strata under the earth. Likewise, these "bombshells" help you measure the hidden layers of addiction within your church.

- Let each individual complete it alone, and then discuss your responses!

- For the daring, use an overhead projector or newsprint to chart the average response from the group to each question!

- For the really daring, chart responses to each question according to age groups: 18 and younger, 19-35, 36-50, 51-65, 66 and older.

27

- For the really, really daring, chart responses to each question according to tenure of membership: less than 6 months, 6 months to 3 years, 3 years to 5 years, 5 years to 10 years, and more than 10 years.

- At the end of the Church Stress Test, score responses in any of the above ways according to key issues for congregational life.

By charting your average stress, you can begin to discern and predict the areas where change will bring you the greatest stress as a congregation.

The Church Stress Test

The following statements are truths about mission that thriving, growing, vital congregations have discovered. They are shocking, because they cause us to confront hidden assumptions and addictive behavior patterns that in the past have blocked the congregation from growth and mission.

The statements below are admittedly extreme, but they contain a core truth for congregational life in the twenty-first century. Let's see where your congregation will feel the most stress in future change! After each statement, identify your personal level of anxiety by assigning a number between 1 and 10. Responses will be gathered during or after two consecutive worship services and averaged. These results will be combined with all the other information being collected in the Congregational Mission Assessment. Go to page 30 and see the *positive* insights of growing churches!

No Anxiety   High Anxiety
1 2 3 4 5 6 7 8 9 10

1. The youth are *not* the future of your church! _____
2. Nobody cares about the *mere* presence of God! _____
3. Every dying church in North America is a friendly congregation! _____
4. There is no such thing as "Good Worship"! _____
5. Most people don't like organ music! _____
6. It doesn't matter what people know following the worship service! _____

28

7. Self-sacrifice is the wrong message! _____
8. Sunday school is no longer the cornerstone of Christian education! _____
9. Church membership is unimportant! _____
10. Jesus does not call you to preserve a heritage! _____
11. More volunteers to fill all the vacancies won't help rescue the church! _____
12. Dutiful service to a church office is a detour on the journey of life! _____
13. Adding professional staff accelerates church decline! _____
14. It is *not* the pastor's job to visit the hospitals! _____
15. Bible study in the church parlor is futile. _____
16. If you want action, *never* form a committee! _____
17. Actions no longer speak louder than words! _____
18. Mission units don't need to report to church boards! _____
19. Debt freedom always leads to church decline! _____
20. Finance committees shouldn't talk about money! _____
21. Unified budgets artificially limit mission! _____
22. Property maintenance is no longer a measure of faithfulness! _____
23. Strategic planning is overrated! _____
24. Building for eternity makes your church obsolete! _____
25. The best leaders make the most mistakes! _____
26. Church *insiders* are the least able to discern future mission! _____
27. Denominational certification has nothing to do with spiritual leadership! _____
28. Sound theology lacks Christian integrity! _____
29. If you can say it all in words, you've missed the point! _____
30. North America is the *least* Christian continent in the world today! _____

Top 30 Positive Discoveries

Compare the positive discovery that corresponds by number with the shocking insight.

1. *Transformed adults (ages 18-40) are the future of your church.*
   Adults who are changed, gifted, called, and equipped will take care of the kids . . . and everything else!

2. *Everybody wants to be touched by the healing and transform-ing power of God.*
   The public is desperate to be changed, different, and liberated from their hurts and addictions.

3. *Thriving, growing churches provide multiple opportunities for safe, healthy intimacy.*
   People want to go beyond the coffee urn to bare their souls with a deeply trusted few.

4. *Worship that works is the only spiritual standard in the post-Christendom world.*
   "Good" worship helps people experience the power of God and walk with Jesus—all else is tactics.

5. *Most people like contemporary music with strong melody and lots of rhythm.*
   Percussion, guitar, creative instrumentations, and small-group ensembles get people's attention.

6. *What matters most is how people feel following the worship service.*
   People want to feel alive for worship, and be motivated to learn and serve through the week.

7. *Self-Affirmation is the right message.*
   People seeking self-worth give generously to express and cele-brate their inner value.

8. *Small groups are the cornerstones of Christian education.*
Groups in any configuration, meeting during the week in homes, promote Christian growth.

9. *Participation in any aspect of congregational life and mission is everything.*
Doing hands-on mission, and involvement in ministry, is more meaningful than mere belonging.

10. *Jesus calls you to risk everything for mission.*
If the past helps you grow Christians for the future, use it. If not, the gospel is all that matters.

11. *Core disciples, who in turn make more disciples, expand God's realm.*
A few people ready to go, grow, and mentor are more effective than many committees.

12. *Excited pursuit of a call brings personal fulfillment.*
People would rather fulfill their destiny than spend their time implementing someone else's agenda.

13. *Growing amateurs to lead ministries from within the congregation grows the church.*
The only reason you add staff is so you can release more gifted, called, and equipped volunteers.

14. *It is the pastoral leader's job to train gifted laity in pastoral care.*
Clergy are trainers, motivators, and visionaries who equip others to do ministries.

15. *On-the-job, biblical action and reflection bear fruit.*
Study the Bible in the physical context of work or mission and reflect on your daily living.

16. *If you want action, find gifted and called individuals and turn them loose.*
Trained laity, who are free to take initiative, will find whatever help they need.

31

17. *You must share your faith motivation for every beneficial service.*
   Evangelism and social action are two sides of the same coin.

18. *Mission units must connect weekly with a worship experience.*
   Today's entrepreneurial teams don't need to get permission, but do need to grow spiritually in worship.

19. *Sound debt management is the key to thriving church development.*
   People will maximize their small investments, and service the debt, of motivating missions.

20. *Finance committees talk about deploying servants.*
   Property and money are resources to be used in the deployment of people for mission.

21. *Capital pools to seed creative ministries multiples mission.*
   Empowered teams take responsibility to raise, manage, and spend the money they need for mission.

22. *Faithfulness is measured by upgradable technologies.*
   Technology is how people discover and interpret meaning in life: upgrade and grow at the same time.

23. *The anticipation of the unpredictable is the art of thriving church life.*
   Spontaneity, flexibility, and planned stress management are part of authentic visions.

24. *Marketability, portability, and flexibility make your church responsive to the mission field.*
   The church building is just a tactic that is always adapted to follow and affect the mission field.

25. *Great leaders intentionally learn from experimentation.*
   An intentional strategy to learn from experimentation is more important than strategic planning.

26. *People on the fringe of church life are key to discerning the future.*
    Biblical visions are most often revealed among those who have been marginalized.

27. *Spiritual leadership speaks out of its own experience of life struggle and spiritual victory.*
    Authenticity is more important than either professional skill or ordination.

28. *Clear Christology is the key to integrity in today's pagan world.*
    All you need to identify is your experience with Jesus that your community cannot live without.

29. *Motivating visions are always a "song in the heart."*
    They are best shared without word, to get the blood of total strangers pounding.

30. *The mission field today is right outside your back door.*
    Today most people in North America are confused or ignorant about even the basics of Christian belief.

Adding Your Addictions, Counting Your Opportunities

Add your scores in each of the following areas. Higher numbers indicate areas where you will find it difficult to understand or implement change. Lower numbers indicate possible "entry points" to initiate church transformation. *Remember, the statements overlap because from one direction or another, sooner or later, transformation touches the whole system of church life.*

Vision and Identity	Statements 1, 3, 10, 26, 29	Average: _____
Worship and Spirituality	Statements 2, 4, 5, 6, 28	Average: _____
Education and Nurture	Statements 7, 8, 12, 15, 28	Average: _____

33

Outreach and Mission	Statements 17, 18, 19, 23, 30	Average: _____
Organization and Structure	Statements 11, 13, 16, 22, 24	Average: _____
Stewardship and Finance	Statements 7, 20, 21, 22, 24	Average: _____
Leadership and Membership	Statements 9, 13, 14, 25, 27	Average: _____

Session 2
Why Do People Yearn for God?

Goal   In this session, we will understand the changing spiritual yearning of the public, and why the gospel is received as "welcome relief."

Prayer Focus   Prior to this session, make an amateur videotape of people in a shopping mall or sports arena. Now play the videotape without sound twice. Watch the first showing without stopping. During the second showing, stop the tape periodically, and ask individuals or table groups to point out a complete stranger in the video for whom they wish to pray.

Discuss briefly why you feel drawn to pray for the stranger in the videotape. Then spend five minutes in silent prayer for that stranger.

Bible Study   Read aloud the story of the acceptance of Zacchaeus in Luke 19:1-11.

People today long for a glimpse of God. They are willing to risk their public image and do silly things, just to experience the Holy. They long for a Higher Power to recognize the good within them, and rescue them from the lifestyles that enslave them. Answer the following questions:

Why do "crowd scenes" attract seekers?

What might Zacchaeus be really looking for?

What is the spiritual significance of Jesus staying at his house?

Why would righteous people grumble at Jesus' decision to eat with Zacchaeus?

What does it mean to be saved in this story?

Now read the story aloud once more. However, when you come to Jesus' words in verses 9-10, shout the words together in unison: *"Today salvation has come to this house, because he too is a son of Abraham. For the Son of Man came to seek out and to save the lost."*

Discussion

Many have compared the postmodern world of the twenty-first century to the premodern world of the first century. The relative place of Christianity in culture today makes this a new apostolic age. Reread the section "It's a First-Century World" (*Kicking Habits,* pages 255-58). Discuss global examples of contemporary events that illustrate the in-between time in which we live:

- Apocalyptic expectations
- Alienation from authority
- Cultic, mystical, and religious experimentation
- Highly competitive and diverse religious market
- Ambiguity and experimentation regarding gender, intimacy, and family life
- Migration of races and peoples, and cross-cultural communication
- Fascination with the irrational and supernatural
- "Feast or Famine" economic changes

- Powerlessness at the hands of hidden, competing tyrants
- Messianic expectations and powerful spiritual yearnings

Once you have identified contemporary events to illustrate the above experiences, tell stories of how you have personally experienced these things.

Which of the five great theological motifs of the apostolic age do you find most relevant to your personal experience—and to the experience of family members, neighbors, and work associates?

1. *Sentinel Theology:* The proclamation of universal, hopeful visions of the future that satisfy our longing for justice, peace, and spiritual clarity.
2. *Healing:* The experience of transformation from physical, relational, mental, emotional, or spiritual brokenness that satisfies our longing to be healthy and whole.
3. *Walking with the Risen Lord:* Constant coaching through the ambiguities of daily living, acceptance of who we are, that satisfies our longing to live a worthy lifestyle.
4. *The return to Eden:* The experience of original purity, and the restoration of environmental perfection, that satisfies our longing to live once again without shame.
5. *The Damascus Road:* The unexpected intervention of a Higher Power that shatters old habits, and satisfies our longing to be born again into a new life.

Think of one person you know and care about *who is not connected with any church.* Circle the two theological motifs that you believe most strongly motivate that person's search for meaning.

Now share your perceptions with others in your group. Take a copy of the following chart to work with you tomorrow, and during the lunch break observe others and complete the chart with your perceptions of them.

- *For the really daring,* check your perceptions with the spouse, friend, or workmate you had in mind.

- *For the really, really daring,* check your perceptions with the work associate that you have been observing!

Exercise

The book *Kicking Habits* offers as a teaching tool—a rather black-and-white comparison between Freda and Fred, and Bob and Sally. Many people find themselves in-between both extremes. Are you more like Freda and Fred, or Bob and Sally? Using a continuum from 1 *(totally Freda and Fred)* to 10 *(totally like Bob and Sally)* place yourself and others on the map of spiritual hunger.

Freda & Fred (1) Value this:	Me	Spouse	Friend	Work Mate	Bob & Sally (10) Value this:
Who I am					Who I can become
Union with traditions					Freedom from addictions
Personal loyalty					Personal integrity
Making sense of the world					Appreciation of universe
Personal history					Personal destiny
Friendship					Intimacy
Happiness					Ecstasy
Follow the cross					*Walk with the risen Lord*

Freda & Fred (1) Behave like this:					Bob & Sally (10) Behave like this:
Restructure society					Transform people
Do good in order to be good					Do good because they are good
Committee work					Personal service
Holiness through righteousness					Righteousness through holiness
Life is moral					Life is ironic
No funny business					Laugh at anything
Confidence in professionals					Confidence in chance
Do it to be like Christ					*Do it to be with Jesus*

II

A BETTER WAY TO BE THE CHURCH!

Read chapters 2-4 of
Kicking Habits (pages 45-113)

Yes! There is a better way to be the church! More and more veteran clergy and laity, and certainly more and more seekers and newcomers, are wearily asking themselves: *Surely there has got to be more to life in the church!* They want more freedom. They want more depth. They want more fulfillment. They want more mission. They want more joy.

The solution to all this is bigger than any particular program, office, or staff position. It involves the whole flow of our experience of congregational life. When you think about "systems" in regard to the church, do not think of a computer system, or a factory assembly line, or a denominational polity, or an ecclesiastical tradition.

- Think of an ecosystem. Think of all the biological factors that are required for a healthy river or a healthy lake to teem with fish, natural wildlife, while maintaining clean and fresh water.
- Think of a family system. Think of all the relational, emotional, cultural, and economic factors that are required to raise a healthy, loving, productive family.
- Think of a human growth system. Think of all the physical, mental, emotional, relational, and spiritual factors that are required for a newborn baby to truly *thrive* and grow.

The phrase "church growth" is a metaphor. It is not an industrial metaphor to describe the multiplication of widgets in the factory. It is not about mere numbers. The phrase "church growth" is a pediatric metaphor to describe how the human organism can grow to have life in abundance.

God does not want the church to be drudgery or a duty that burns people out. God wants the church to be an experience of joy that helps people discover themselves and fulfill their lives in the mission field as disciples of Jesus. God does not want the church to just take care of its members, but to empower church members to fulfill their individual and corporate life destiny by reaching out to become a blessing to all humankind. The result of the former may be friendship, happiness, and harmony. The result of the latter will be intimacy, ecstasy, and joy.

Before you launch into the next five sessions, take time to read and discuss the following scripture passage, and complete the following exercise. Stand back and survey your life experience in the congregations in which you have participated. Then reflect on the flow of your experience in *this* particular congregation.

Bible
Study
Read the story of Pentecost in Acts 2:1-17, and 36-47.

Describe in your own words the process through which the apostles and early Christians were transformed from timid seekers to bold disciples.

Exercise
The key metaphors for the declining and thriving church systems identify the "core process" that is intentionally or unintentionally experienced be every member of the church.

The Croquet Game	*The Jai Alai Game*
Going through the hoops, people are: enrolled, informed, nominated, supervised, and kept.	Racing through the air, people are: changed, gifted, called, equipped, sent.

Rate your experience in each of the five categories by writing a number from 1 to 5 in the middle column, with "1" being most like a croquet game of going through the hoops, and "5" being most like a jai alai game of racing through the air. What is your intuition? Do you experience church as being—

40

Croquet	1, 2, 3, 4, 5	Jai Alai
Enrolled: I'm always fulfilling membership duties, pledging money, accepting tasks, and sacrificing myself for the church.	My Rating:	*Changed:* I'm always experiencing my life and lifestyle being shaped and reshaped in unexpected and positive ways by God.
Informed: I'm always being taught correct ideology or pure dogma, or absorbing institutional or denominational information.	My Rating:	*Gifted:* I'm always finding and improving spiritual gifts, deepening self-knowledge, building profound trust, and discovering Jesus again.
Nominated: I'm always serving offices, meeting in committees, managing budgets, and doing things others believe to be important.	My Rating:	*Called:* I'm always listening to hear God's mission for me and my church to fulfill ourselves in local/ global outreach that we know to be vital.
Supervised: I'm always writing or reading reports, evaluating programs, and telling or being told what to do.	My Rating:	*Equipped:* I'm always upgrading my skills and awareness, questing for excellence, and learning to be the best servant of God I can be.
Kept: I'm always sacrificing creativity for harmony, visiting church members, preserving heritage, overcoming deficits, and eager for summer holidays.	My Rating:	*Sent:* I'm always with my team, through the week, doing great stuff for others and talking about my faith, living life abundantly, and eager to worship every single week.

41

Discuss the following questions:

Which core process do you experience in your church?

If your experience is a little of both, describe how you experience the two metaphors—as a source of empowerment or as a source of conflict?

Does your congregation observe *Pentecost or* do *Pentecost?*

Session 1
Do You Want to Change People or Enroll Newcomers?

Goal   In this session, we will clarify and build the right attitude toward newcomers, and the best strategies for worship, which will help our church become an experience of joy and a blessing to humankind.

Prayer Focus   Find one or more old photographs of the construction of your church building. Imagine what it must have felt like to be a part of that project. Ask God to revive the passion, daring, hope, and mission spirit that was in the hearts of people in those days.

Bible Study   Read aloud the story of the healed paralytic in Luke 5:17-26. There is a deep urgency about the gospel today, and an urgency that is felt by people like Bob and Sally who long for the touch of the Holy. This urgency is often missing from the worship experience of declining churches. Discuss the following questions:

Why should *busy people feel any urgency to come to worship in your church?*

Which is more important: to be forgiven or to rise up and walk? If both are important, can you do one without trying to do the other? How does your church do it?

When was the last time in worship that amazement seized the participants, and they left in animated conversation saying, "We have seen strange things today"?

Now read the story aloud once more, and when you come to the last phrase shout aloud: *"We have seen strange things today."*

Discussion

There is an old saying about accountability: *"You made your bed, now you have to lie in it!"* If postmodern people come to church today, they are motivated by this deep sense of entrapment. It is not that they want to escape responsibility, or that they resent being held responsible, but that they sense at the deepest level that the power to change does not lie within them. They long for the touch of the Holy. Only Jesus can say "rise, even from the bed you have made, walk and be free!" A specific "Christ focus" is crucial to worship today.

Declining churches greet newcomers at the door and wonder: *What can this newcomer do to support our church programs?* They want you to join the church. Thriving churches greet newcomers

43

and wonder: *How can we help you fulfill your destiny with Christ?* They want to change people, society, and the world.

Here is the key question for transformation. Answer it as individuals and as a group.

What is it about your experience with Jesus that this community cannot live without?

Exercise

Discuss your answers to the following questions from the *Congregational Mission Assessment*. (For future reference, the numbers following each question correspond to the numbering in *Facing Reality: A Congregational Mission Assessment Tool*).

In ten words or less, what is the core message you continually project beyond the church? (109)

What is the benefit that people receive from each worship service? (33)

(NOTE: Record the average score from each worksheet on a 1-10 scale with "1" being extremely negative and "10" being extremely positive. Duplicate for additional services if necessary.)

Service	Personal Transformational Factor	Personal Support Factor	Motivation for Spiritual Growth Factor	Education and Learning Factor	Mission Connection Factor
1					
2					
3					
4					

What are your three most memorable experiences (positive or negative) from worship services in the past year? (38)

a) What happened?
b) Why was it so memorable?
c) How did it affect the lifestyles of others?

Declining churches believe that good worship must be done in specific ways, with only certain kinds of music, in an essentially unchanging environment of seating and symbols. Thriving churches believe that the only good worship is worship that helps strangers experience the transforming power of God and walk daily with Jesus. Everything else is mere tactics.

If you adopted the philosophy of the thriving church, how would that change your worship patterns?

Who do you think might come to church for the first time, and how do you need to prepare to receive them?

Who do you think would leave the church, and how would you faithfully cope with the stress of losing them?

Session 2
Do You Want to Grow Disciples or Inform Members?

Goal

In this session, we will underline the importance of spiritual growth *for adults*, and clarify thriving church assumptions about membership and the time management of leaders.

Prayer Focus

Place a very large picture frame where all can see it. Let the frame be ornate, and the matting be colorful, but *no* picture should be in the frame. Ask each individual to remember the mentor who most powerfully influenced his or her spiritual development. Imaginatively place this person's face in the frame. Meditate on the qualities and lifestyle of that person, and the impact the person had on your life.

Bible Study

Read aloud the story of the disciples' encounter with Jesus on the Emmaus road in Luke 24:13-32. The North American public feels a deep need to learn and grow. Continuing education and self-help programs are more popular than ever before. Yet declining churches are now the remnant of the population who are *not* on a high learning curve! In declining churches, less than 2 to 5 percent of the laity are involved in any intentional spiritual growth discipline during the week.

What were the key themes or ideas that Cleopas and his friend needed to hear?

What were the key methods or processes through which Cleopas and his friend eventually recognized Jesus?

What does it mean to have a "burning heart," and when did your heart last burn?

Now read verses 31-34 aloud, and when you come to verse 34 shout together the following phrase, *inserting the name of your mentor whom you have remembered*: *"The Lord has risen indeed, and he has appeared to _____."*

Discussion

Thriving churches believe that God uniquely gifts every human being. Each person is created in a special way with the potential to be a blessing to all humankind. If individuals discern and use those gifts, they will find joy and fulfillment in life. Thriving churches are not content to simply inform people about the needs of the church institution (for finances or committee service or correct dogma). They believe membership is a covenant to go deep into one's fundamental values and beliefs, to discover themselves, the nature of healthy relationships, and the fullness of God.

What are the expectations of membership in your church?

How does your church help adults form partnerships to support and help one another in spiritual growth?

How much time each week do you want your pastor (or pastoral team) to spend with adults who seriously and intentionally want to go deeper in their spiritual lives? (NOTE: You may want to ask

47

the pastor or pastoral team to think about this and respond to your perceptions separately.)

Exercise   Discuss your answers to the following questions from the *Congregational Mission Assessment.*

Describe a time of crisis or confusion. What person within the church who is not on the church staff helped you resolve or overcome it? (42)

A Time of Crisis	The Person in the Church Who Helped Me

Rate the importance of these expectations of membership in the church. (42) (1 — high, 2 — medium, 3 — low)

a) Regular worship attendance ____
b) Percentage giving ____
c) Tithing ____
d) Spiritual disciplines ____

e) Cell-group participation ____
f) Personal mission involvement ____
g) Public confession of faith ____
h) Organizational leadership ____

Other Expectations:_____

Declining churches are obsessed with youth groups and children's programs, but fail to understand that their struggle to do these things cannot be solved by better programs, curriculums, or magnetic pastors. Thriving churches understand that only when adults become serious about spiritual growth themselves will the church have lasting and effective youth and children's ministries.

If you adopted this philosophy of growth, how would that change your budgeting and leadership deployment strategies?

Why do you think adults in your church might hesitate to become involved in disciplines for spiritual growth, and what can you do about it?

How will your pastor and church staff need to reprioritize their energies in order to motivate and encourage widespread participation of adult laity in spiritual growth?

Session 3
Do You Want to Fulfill Lives or Fill Offices?

Goal

In this session, we will understand the link between Christian maturity and Christian ministry, and clarify thriving church assumptions about mission discernment and lay ministries.

Prayer Focus

Make a collage of six large photographs, chosen both for relevance to specific missions and also as metaphors for mission in general. Under each photograph print boldly the phrases *"I was hungry," "I was thirsty," "I was a stranger," "I was naked," "I was sick,"* and *"I was in prison."* Meditate on the collage of photographs, and let your stream of consciousness draw your heart toward local and global examples of mission in each category.

Bible Study

Read aloud the story of the calling of Aquila, Priscilla, and Apollos in Acts 18:1-3, 18, 24-28. Research and discuss their different cultural and economic backgrounds.

What is the difference between a call and a task?

Now read 1 Corinthians 1:26-31. Share with one another your personal, unique sense of calling. Share your anxieties over your ability to fulfill your call.

What is the difference between celebration of your call, and egotism?

Now read 1 Corinthians 3:5-9. Discuss how your call is supportive of, or supported by, the call of others. Read aloud again 1 Corinthians 1:30, 31, and shout aloud the final words: *Let the one who boasts, boast in the Lord.*

50

Discussion

Thriving churches believe that God calls every Christian into ministry. The discernment of this ministry, however, is not the responsibility of the board or staff of the church. It is discovered only in conversation between each individual Christian and God. No one can tell you what it is that will fulfill your destiny. You must discern that for yourself.

Therefore, the mission agenda of the thriving church does not arise from the strategic planning of a church institution, but rather from the spiritual growth of the people. It is the individuals who have heard their call who will inform the church leaders about the future mission of the church, and the responsibility of the church to help people fulfill their destiny in Christ.

What missions or ministries in your church emerged from the spiritual growth of the people who lead those ministries?

What missions or ministries in your church were assigned to the church by the board or denomination, which then recruited people to implement these missions?

If you shift mission development to become a function of spiritual growth, rather than strategic planning, how will this change your budgeting process?

Exercise

Discuss your answers to the following questions from the *Congregational Mission Assessment.*

List three creative ideas that emerged spontaneously in congregational life over the past five years, which did not emerge from a strategic plan or committee meeting? (42)

This is the creative idea —	*and this is what happened to that idea!*

How do congregational leaders intentionally listen to marginal members and the spiritually yearning, institutionally alienated, public? (58)

What method does the congregation use to learn from mistakes or failures? (56)

How do staff members help others discern their own calling or ministry? (60)

(NOTE: Focus on intentional disciplines or repeatable methods.)

How does the pastor do it?

How do the program staff or volunteer leaders do it?

How the support staff or volunteers do it?

Declining churches recruit people with needed talents into the committees and task groups of the church. The church borrows their skills to fulfill the institution's agenda. Thriving churches help people discern their gifts and callings, and empower them to fulfill themselves in the pursuit of their mission.

52

If your church were to adopt this policy, how would it change your nominations and staff development strategies?

What conflicts would that precipitate with your denominational judicatory, and how would you resolve them?

What gaps in mission or ministry might emerge, and how would you address these?

Session 4
Do You Want to Equip Ministers or Supervise Committees?

Goal

In this session, we will understand the need to finance, train, and coach volunteer ministries, and clarify thriving church assumptions about the role of clergy.

Prayer Focus

Borrow a sign or slogan from one of any number of small or large businesses that seek to emphasize quality. You can find such signs on the walls of many small businesses in your community. Place the sign where it is very visible. Meditate on how it motivates or guides those who manage or work in small businesses or nonprofit organizations.

Bible Study

Read aloud James 1:19-25 and 2:14-17. As you read, let one person in the group keep a list of all references to positive attitudes or behavior patterns that disciples of Christ should have. Discuss your answers to these questions.

What attitudes or behavior patterns would be most difficult for you personally to attain?

Imagine that your church is like a small business competing for the attention of the world, and you are the manager. How would you train your staff to have the best attitudes and abilities to do their work?

Remember the calling that you identified in the earlier session. What skills do you need to fulfill that call in the best manner possible? How will you obtain those skills?

Discussion

Thriving churches help people become *doers* of ministry, not merely administrators of ministry. They have large continuing education budgets for volunteers. The staff members spend much of their time training and coaching people to do ministries they believe God calls them to do. Declining churches only ask members to raise money to pay professionals to do mission. Thriving churches know that volunteers will not find fulfillment in life sitting in church basements or parlors thinking about, planning, or supervising mission. Volunteers will find fulfillment in life only in doing mission themselves locally and globally.

Review the list of skills needed to fulfill the callings from the Bible study. What budget do you need in the church to train people in these skills with high quality?

How can you regularly recognize, commission, pray for, and support the doers of ministry in your church?

How can you free staff, or how can you find the coaches, so that volunteers can be trained with the attitudes and skills necessary for quality ministries?

Exercise

Discuss your answers to the following questions from the *Congregational Mission Assessment.*

How do social service missions from the congregation communicate their faith motivation to the general public? (66)

How does the congregation train volunteers to work sensitively with other cultures, ethnic groups, or minorities in their local community or global partnerships? (67)

How much time and energy does the pastor give to empowering lay ministries? (70) (NOTE: Record the average score from each worksheet on a 1-10 scale as indicated below. You may wish to invite the clergy to complete this chart separately and then compare perceptions.)

	To What Degree is the pastor doing ministry alone (1) or mentoring apprentices to do that ministry (10)?	To what degree is the pastor doing tasks in behalf of the church (1) or training others to do the same work (10)?	To what degree is the pastor counseling with individuals (1) or coaching groups (10)?
Your Perspective			
Clergy Perspective			

Declining churches prioritize volunteer energy to raise money in order to pay others to do mission. Therefore, they become preoccupied with issues of *control*, so that they can ensure that money is spent properly and mission employees do what they are told to do. Thriving churches prioritize training and coaching, because quality work is the best way to trust the integrity, innovation, and initiative of volunteers.

If your church were to adopt this priority, what committees would become unnecessary?

If your staff were to prioritize training and coaching others for ministries, rather than doing it themselves, how would your staff need to retrain?

How will you respond to angry parishioners who see the shift in roles played by the clergy, and feel that the clergy are no longer "doing what we hired them to do"?

Session 5
Do You Want to Deploy Servants or Keep Everybody Happy?

Goal
In this session, we will discern the importance of team mission, and ponder the reality that in the past and present apostolic age, the harmony of church insiders was secondary to bringing hope to the world.

Prayer Focus
Set side by side a large picture of the earth (preferably from a perspective that does not place North America in the center), and an aerial picture of your village, town, or city. Imagine that you are a dove flying over all the earth, yet seeing every individual, carrying a morsel of grace to address human need. Where will you land? Where does your heart lead you to settle, to bring a blessing to humankind?

Bible Study
Read aloud the story of the mission of the Seventy in Acts 10:1-12. Then read aloud the commissioning of Paul and Barnabas in Acts 13:1-3. Circle or note any verses that are confusing or unsettling, and discuss these verses first. Now discuss your answers to the following questions:

The central metaphor of the entire passage is the harvest and the laborers. Therefore, the reference to carrying no purse, bag, or sandals is also a metaphor. What are the material things that are holding you back from being with Jesus in the mission field?

Laborers in the field are so focused on the harvest that they haven't time for idle conversation ("greeting people on the road"). What are the idle conversations, or fruitless meetings, that are distracting your church from being with Jesus in the mission field?

There is a sense of urgency in this story—and in the mission field of today. Time is not on our side.

Why is time running out for the church to be with Jesus in the mission field?

Discussion

Thriving churches always equip and send *teams* of two or more people to do any and every mission or ministry. These teams simultaneously do good, and articulate their faith motivation for doing it. The members of the church feel such urgency about mission that they feel more restless than content. Declining churches prize internal harmony above all. They do nothing risky or daring, for fear that just one member might not like it. Declining churches send people home to Sunday lunch. Thriving churches send people out to a week of spiritual growth and daring service.

Why is your Christian faith so crucial to your life that the good works you do would never get done unless you were a believer in Jesus Christ?

What difference would it really make to your community or to the world if your local congregation closed tomorrow? Name five things that could not possibly happen unless your congregation existed.

Exercise

Discuss your answers to the following questions from the *Congregational Mission Assessment.*

How many visitors to worship came as a result of a particular mission or ministry of the church? (73) (Estimate percentage of total worshipers per year.)

Does worship regularly focus prayer or celebration on one or more of the above missions or ministries? (74)

58

Does the church create a welcome and inclusive environment for the lifestyle diversity of the public? (79)

Declining churches recruit people to implement someone else's agenda. Thriving churches deploy true teams that have the power to discern, design, implement, and evaluate mission without asking permission. Declining churches waste time as ad hoc committees make decisions. Thriving churches rapidly respond to emerging mission needs.

Are volunteers in your church generally deployed as "teams" or "task groups"? (76)

Circle the number in each continuum that best describes how volunteer groups are deployed. You may wish to do this individually, then compare your responses.

TRUE TEAMS	*Circle the number in each category*		*TASK GROUPS*
Discern emerging mission by itself	1 2 3 4 5	6 7 8 9 10	Recruited to address mission perceived by board or clergy
Design strategies to address mission on its own	1 2 3 4 5	6 7 8 9 10	Told how to address the mission
Implement mission strategies without asking permission	1 2 3 4 5	6 7 8 9 10	Submit recommended strategies for approval
Evaluate mission results on its own	1 2 3 4 5	6 7 8 9 10	Submit reports to board or clergy for evaluation
Do both social action and faith witness	1 2 3 4 5	6 7 8 9 10	Do tasks without articulating faith motivation
Leaders emerge from spiritual growth processes of congregation	1 2 3 4 5	6 7 8 9 10	Leader nominated or appointed by administrative meeting

III

ESCAPING THE TORNADO OF CHURCH DECLINE!

Read chapters 5-6 of
Kicking Habits (pages 121-75)

Yes! You can escape the tornado of church decline! But in order to do it, you must experience a tidal wave of God's grace! Either way, you can be certain that the future holds two things for you and your congregation:

1. *The future will be stressful.* Tornadoes suck you down, down, down into a vortex of demoralization and despair that eventually leads to aging memberships and eventual closure. Tidal waves carry you away, away, away in directions you never expected, which eventually lead to surprising joy and mission challenges.

2. *The future will not be entirely in your control.* Both tornadoes and tidal waves have a will of their own, and the best laid strategic plans will come to nothing. In a tornado, you walk by daydreaming, not by planning. In a tidal wave, you walk by faith and not by sight.

The tornado of church decline looks like this:

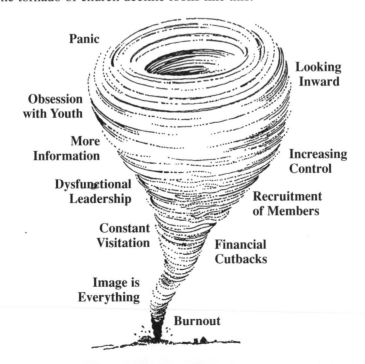

Panic

Looking Inward

Obsession with Youth

More Information

Increasing Control

Dysfunctional Leadership

Recruitment of Members

Constant Visitation

Financial Cutbacks

Image is Everything

Burnout

If you feel that you are declining, circle what you perceive to be your current location in the tornado of church decline. Remember, the deeper you are in the tornado, the more difficult and the more stressful it will be to get out again.

The tidal wave of grace looks like this:

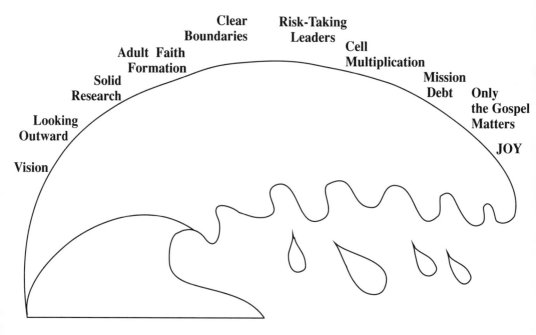

Faith-Sharing
Service

Clear
Boundaries

Risk-Taking
Leaders

Cell
Multiplication

Adult Faith
Formation

Solid
Research

Mission
Debt

Only
the Gospel
Matters

Looking
Outward

JOY

Vision

In order to surf the tidal wave of grace, you eventually need a new organizational model that can experience stress positively, and take risks with integrity.

Before you launch into the next four sessions, take time to read and discuss the following scripture passage, and complete the following exercise. Consider how you personally, and your congregation as a whole, have dealt with change in the past. Change is always stressful, but people find some aspects of change more difficult than others.

Bible Study	Read the story of the rebuilding of the Temple, and especially Nehemiah 8:9-10. Describe in your own words how the Israelites returning from exile found strength to overcome obstacles, create new traditions, fulfill the lives of the refugees, and rediscover the true meaning of faithfulness.
Exercise	In the tidal wave of positive change, where do you anticipate the greatest stress for yourself as a leader, and for the congregation as a whole? Rate your stress level from 1 (low) to 5 (high).
Daring:	Share your scores with others in your group and talk about them.
More daring:	Average the responses from your group together. Discuss why certain stages will be so stressful, and ponder how you can address the stress.
Really daring:	Trade your group's average scores with those of another group chosen at random. Compare and discuss.
Totally daring:	Average the scores of all the groups, and ask community groups (youth, seniors, ethnic minorities, and others) to give you feedback.

Stage in the Wave of Positive Change	My Anticipated Stress	My Expectation of Congregational Stress
Vision: Individuals receiving, sharing, owning, and proclaiming visions of hope that, like all biblical visions, may sear your lips, dislocate your hip, or change your name.		
Looking Outward: Prioritizing the need to listen to, pray for, and address the "spiritually yearning, institutionally alienated public" who are the "Gentiles" of the new apostolic age.		
Solid Research: Demographic research to obtain facts and perspectives on the real attitudes, behavior, and expectations of people inside and beyond the church.		
Adult Faith Formation: Priority of budget and energy for adult spiritual growth that is partnered in triads or small groups, guided by spiritual leaders, and is a daily walk with Jesus.		
Clear Boundaries: Development of clear congregational consensus regarding the core values, bedrock beliefs, motivating vision, and key mission transparent in the behavior of members.		

Continued . . .

Stage in the Wave of Positive Change	My Anticipated Stress	My Expectation of Congregational Stress
Faith-Sharing Service: Team-based volunteer ministries that do simultaneous evangelism and social action, that involve more and more members in hands-on mission.		
Risk-Taking Leaders: Daring leaders who are prepared to take initiative, are unafraid of failure, are ready to learn from mistakes, are committed to outreach, and are focused on Christ above all.		
Cell Multiplication: Constantly changing partnerships of people, eager to go deep, hear call, do mission, and then close the cell and start all over again mentoring a new group.		
Mission Debt: Readiness to develop faith-based budgets, constantly and wisely manage mission-driven debt, give options for designated giving, and invest in God's future.		
Only the Gospel: Readiness to treat the gospel alone as sacred, and to regard literally everything else about the church program, property, and leadership as tactics that can be changed.		
Joy: Preference to live in creative instability, rather than contented harmony, openness to the irrational inbreaking of God's Spirit and God's Mission, serenity in placing one's personal and institutional life in God's hands alone.		

Where will people in your group likely feel the most stress in the tidal wave of positive change?

Where do you think the congregation as a whole might experience the most stress?

Session 1
The Energy Field

Goal

In this session we will understand how thriving churches build clarity and consensus about congregational identity, and thus provide boundaries that are an incentive to creativity and a foundation of trust.

Prayer Focus

Obtain a simple science project from the local high school that illustrates how a spinning coil surrounded by a magnetic field powers an electric motor. Watch the motor run. Stop and start the motor several times.

Remember times when you felt the Holy Spirit move invisibly in the church (or in your heart) like an electrical charge.

What are the boundaries of core values and beliefs that guide your daily activities, shape your spontaneity, and empower your creativity?

Bible Study

Read *silently* the story of the Jerusalem Council in Acts 15:1-11, 19-21. Then read aloud Paul's guidance to the unruly Corinthian church in

1 Corinthians 1:18-25, and his articulation of the fruits of the Spirit in Galatians 5:22-26. Discuss your answers to these questions:

Stated in more positive language, what are the expectations of the Jerusalem Council for the faith and practice of new Gentile Christians?

Why can't the "fruits of the Spirit" be replaced by a denominational polity as a vehicle for accountability?

Now read aloud the passage from Galatians once more. However, when you come to verse 25, shout the words together in unison: *"If we live by the Spirit, let us also be guided by the Spirit."*

Discussion

Thriving churches have enormous clarity and consensus about their shared core values, beliefs, and vision. They have devoted time and energy to go deep, build conversation, own faith for themselves, and articulate that identity to the public. Declining churches live in a fog about their congregational identity. They rely on liturgical readings in worship (that only the clergy really understand) to articulate their beliefs, and allow matriarchs or patriarchs to impose boundaries of creativity based on personal tastes and political preferences.

This is why declining churches tend to be very homogeneous, even though they claim to be "inclusive." Those people who are really allowed into the inner core of congregational management all resemble the matriarchs and patriarchs. On the other hand, thriving churches are very heterogeneous, and mirror the demographic diversity of the

67

surrounding community. The personal preferences of leaders become secondary to the shared core values, beliefs, and vision that is the real "energy field" of church life.

One thriving congregation gives away T-shirts to every new member, worship leader, staff member, and other visitors to the church. On the front of the T-shirt are the top ten core values they expect their people will model in everyday life as Christians. On the back of the T-shirt are the top ten core beliefs they expect their people will turn to whenever they are in trouble. Their vision is a song that they sing every time they gather for fellowship or worship, which sends shivers up and down the spines of participants. *If you were to do the same tactic, what would* you *do?*

What key words or phrases would you write on the front of the T-shirt that would clearly communicate the core values that you expect church members to model in daily living?

What key words or images would you place on the back of the T-shirt that would clearly communicate the core beliefs that give you strength to overcome any trouble?

What song would you sing as a congregation that reveals your supreme vision as a congregation to follow Jesus into the mission field that sends shivers up and down the spines of the participants whenever they sing it?

Are you, personally, prepared to wear that T-shirt to work, to play, at home, and among your neighbors? (Circle the number on the continuum that best reveals your own commitment then compare your responses with others.)

No! I would never have the audacity to reveal my Christian identity that way.	1 2 3 4 5 6 7 8 9 10	Yes! I would always take every opportunity to reveal my Christian identity that way.

Exercise

Discuss your answers to the following questions from the *Congregational Mission Assessment*. (For future reference, numbers following each question correspond to the numbering in *Facing Reality: A Congregational Mission Assessment Tool*.)

NOTE: For an in-depth understanding of core values, beliefs, vision, and mission, and a process of building congregational clarity and consensus, see *Moving Off the Map: A Field Guide to Changing the Congregation* by Thomas G. Bandy (Nashville: Abingdon Press, 1998).

What are the core values, beliefs, and vision of your congregation? (5, 6, 7)

Our Core Values	*Our Core Beliefs*	*Our Vision*
1.		
2.		
3.		
4.		
5.		

Mission Statement who can quote it

How do you intentionally communicate the core values, beliefs, and vision of the congregation to newcomers, visitors, and the general public? (9, 10)

In your perspective, do the leaders of your congregation (including staff, board members, and lay leaders of groups and educational programs) readily articulate the core values, beliefs, and vision of the congregation, and also model these in daily behavior? (12, 13, 14)

(NOTE: You may wish to follow this process to reduce stress:

a) Circle the number on the continuum that best reveals your own perspective
b) Average the responses from your table group or small group
c) Ask individual leaders to do their work separately, and average their responses
d) Compare the responses without reference to individual leaders.)

NO! Leaders don't readily articulate or model this identity.   1 2 3 4 5 6 7 8 9 10   *YES! Leaders do readily articulate and model this identity.*

Do a simple market survey of those people who rent or use your property through the week, but who do not attend your church. Choose the two evenings when your building is most in use. Position teams of two people beside the major entrances during times when people come and go. Equip them with clipboards to record results. In a friendly and nonaggressive manner they should ask people for just a few seconds of their time to respond to a survey that will help the church. Here are the questions:

1. Positively or negatively, how would you describe the people of this church?

2. What do you think are the most important beliefs of this church?

3. At the present time, do you regularly participate in a church or religious organization?

4. If you were to participate in a church, what is the most important thing you would look for?

Do this for several weeks. Collate the results. Compare the perceptions of the public with your own understanding of your core values, beliefs, and vision. *Do you feel affirmed or challenged?*

Session 2
The Circle of Life

Goal

In this session we will understand the difference between "participation" and "membership," and how the thriving church organizes itself around affinity groups rather than committees.

Prayer Focus

Obtain a lava lamp or bubble light from a novelty store. (These are table lamps illuminating a liquid core in which heated air bubbles or doughy globs continually rise to the surface.) Darken the room and stare at the lamp. See how the bubbles form, rise, fall, and rise again in unpredictable ways. Imagine the Holy Spirit heating the spiritual gifts and callings of people, so that they rise up to do mission in unpredictable ways, and realign with new partners to continually form new mission opportunities.

Bible Study

Read aloud the personal greeting of Paul to the house church of Prisca and Aquila in Romans 16:1-16. Go ahead and wrestle with the pronunciation of the names of individuals, just as people today have wrestled with the correct pronunciation of your own name! Note the various ways each individual is uniquely defined and loved. If you wish, do additional research into the origins of the house church in apostolic times.

Why does the proper pronunciation of a name matter to every individual?

How would you describe yourself (or want to be known to others) based on your:

a) gifts and abilities;
b) relationships with others;
c) mission and work?

71

Have you ever been part of a small group where you felt as valued, loved, and encouraged toward self-fulfillment, as appears in this Roman house church? Describe to others what it was like.

Discussion

Thriving churches want people to become involved in a deepening relationship with Jesus Christ. Whether or not people join the church is secondary. They want people to enter into covenant partnerships with a small number of others where there is an environment in which individuals can go deeper into themselves, their relationships, and their experience of God.

People grow best in the company of others who cherish and encourage them. This company is small in number so that each participant can interact intimately with others. It is not based on a curriculum, a program, or an agenda, but rather on a shared affinity. An "affinity" is any shared concern or enthusiasm, about any imaginable topic, issue, or activity.

Traditional committees differ from such small groups in many ways. Committees are recruited around an imposed agenda, not a shared affinity. People are elected or appointed, often because they represent another body. They submerge their personal needs for the sake of accomplishing a given task. If they bond together, or grow closer to God, these are secondary matters. What is important to a committee is that it accomplishes what a governing body wants it to do.

Affinity groups become environments for personal, relational, and spiritual growth when they have a certain structure, described in *Kicking Habits* as PALS:

a) A readiness to pray for one another and for strangers beyond the group;

b) A shared affinity or activity that they not

72

only enjoy, but that can become a vehicle to benefit others beyond the group;

c) A commitment to learn more about themselves, their relationships, and God;

d) A willingness to reveal, risk, and invest themselves in one another so that they build deep, healthy, safe intimacy.

Have you ever been part of a committee, choir, or task group that began to be like a PALS group until the process was halted abruptly so that the group could address a particular agenda or task that was supposedly the point of the group? How did you feel?

Remember our previous discussion in part 1. Why do Fred and Freda prefer committees? Why do Bob and Sally prefer PALS groups? What do you prefer, and why?

Exercise

Discuss your answers to the following questions from the *Congregational Mission Assessment.*

NOTE: For an in-depth understanding of PALS group organization, see *Christian Chaos: Revolutionizing the Congregation* by Thomas G. Bandy (Nashville: Abingdon Press, 1999).

What opportunities does your congregation provide for adult personal, relational, and spiritual growth? (45)

Opportunity	Who provides leadership?	How many people involved in last twelve months?
Spiritual Gifts Discernment		
Personality Inventories		
Lifestyle Coaching		
Mental Health		
Emotional Health		
Life Skills Development		
Pre-Marriage Counseling		
Intimacy Enrichment		
Parenting		
Fellowship		
12-Step Support		
Mission Awareness		
Bible Study		
Faith Formation		
Other Affinities 1. 2. 3. 4.		

The organization described in *Kicking Habits* surrenders centralized control of the mission agenda of the church, and builds church strategies around the needs of the public rather than the expectations of church members. Discuss the following two quotations from pages 148-49 of *Kicking Habits:*

> 1. *It is the public that controls the manner and pace of its involvement with the church—not the institution.*

74

2. It is the individual participant who controls the manner and pace of action and witness with the community—not the institution.

If your church were to adopt such an attitude toward mission, how would that new attitude change your board meetings?

Session 3
The Stability Triangle

Goal

In this session we will discern how power is exercised differently in the thriving church, and understand the streamlined management strategy of the organization.

Prayer Focus

Place a three-legged stool where everyone can see it. Stack a number of dishes on top of it. Make sure that they are *breakable* dishes. Appreciate the value and fragility of the stacked dishes. Admire the balance of the three-legged stool.

Now gather twenty balls of various sizes and cluster them together on the floor. Place a board on top of the balls. Stack another set of *breakable* dishes on top of the board. Imagine that the balls may unexpectedly grow larger or smaller at any time.

Now gather a group of people in a circle that includes both tableaus. Ask these people to jump up and down for several seconds. Meditate silently on the nature and focus of your anxiety.

Bible Study

Read aloud the story of the emerging organization of the apostolic church in Acts 2:43-47; 4:32-35; and 6:1-4. Organization emerged from continuing chaos of life in the spirit.

What are some of the principles or assumptions that shaped the emerging organization?

75

What grounded and guided the exercise of power in the early church?

Why doesn't the early church ever vote on anything?

Discussion

Thriving churches are both purpose driven and exceedingly pragmatic. They will do whatever it takes to deliver the gospel to the world. They want to spiritually nurture, equip, send, support, and resource the greatest number of people to be with Jesus in the mission field. Therefore, they want to tie up the fewest number of people in administration.

Declining churches tie up an enormous number of people in administration and supervision, through innumerable committees and offices, and actually release very few missions into the world.

Thriving churches are so focused on outreach that they are always scrambling to reshape the organization to keep up with the mission. Declining churches are so focused on maintenance that they never find courage or energy to take mission risks.

The organization of the thriving church requires three teams to bring stability to the ongoing chaos of mission. The truth is that in the chaos of emerging mission, you never quite know what tasks each team should be doing. The best you can do is make sure the people on the team are trustworthy (gifted, called, and equipped) and given clear boundaries for their creativity. How might your congregation streamline organization?

1) The Human Resources Team, the mission of which is to grow mature Christians.

What are the gifts, callings, and skills required to do this?

What are the policies or guidelines for their work that would provide maximum freedom and accountability?

2) The Training Team, the mission of which is to equip ministers.

What are the gifts, callings, and skills required to do this?

What are the policies or guidelines for this team's work that would provide maximum freedom and accountability?

3) The Administration Team, the mission of which is to deploy disciples.

What are the gifts, callings, and skills required to do this?

What are the policies or guidelines for this team's work that would provide maximum freedom and accountability?

Exercise   Discuss your answers to the following questions from the *Congregational Mission Assessment*.

Do property and financial managers in your church understand their jobs as "the maintenance of church assets" or "the resourcing of congregational mission"? (81, 91)

(NOTE: You may wish to follow this process to reduce stress:

1. Circle the number on the continuum that best reveals your own perspective;

2. Average the responses from your table group or small group;

3. Ask individual leaders to do their work separately, and average their responses;

4. Compare the responses without reference to individual leaders.)

Purely the maintenance   1 2 3 4 5 6 7 8 9 10   *Purely the resourcing*
of church assets   *of congregational mission*

List all of the missions and ministries related to your congregation and check off how church members related to them. (71)

Mission or Ministry	Property Use Only (Free Use or Rental)	Financial Support Only	Church Members Set Policy	Church Members Participate "Hands-On" in the Mission	Approx. Number of Church Members Involved	Staff or Church Leaders Involved

Remember the prayer focus using the three-legged stool and breakable dishes? Now place the stool on a moveable cart. Fill the dishes with liquid and solid foods, and stack them on the stool. Create an obstacle course in the room.

Divide the group in two. On one end of the room are the Christians with the food cart. At the other end are the publics with any and all needs, yearning for all aspects of the gospel. They are hungry, thirsty, lonely, sick, imprisoned, and so forth.

Let individuals take turns pushing or pulling the cart (stool, dishes, food, etc.), through the obstacle course, to arrive safely to those in need.

Now talk about church leadership.

What did it feel like to have such responsibility?

Were you more afraid of breaking dishes or failing to deliver the goods?

How would you feel if people across the room were dying, while the people with the cart debated about who would go?

Did the people who watched want to help? Did they want to pray? Did they feel intense involvement in the safe delivery of the food cart?

How did it feel when, after perhaps several failures and some broken dishes, the food cart actually arrived at the destination?

What kind of leadership is required for this new organizational model?

Session 4
The Core of Spirituality

Goal

In this session we will begin to understand why worship and spirituality lie at the center of organizational life in the thriving church.

Prayer Focus

Obtain a videotape of a worship service in your church that many believe to be one of best in their experience. Edit the videotape, eliminating all announcements, miscellaneous introductions of people or hymns, wasted time between actions, and so on. Reduce the videotape to the absolute essentials of worship. Now show the videotape to the group. Encourage people to note whatever words, images, sounds, or experiences were most moving for them.

Meditate silently on the question, "Why would I ever allow myself to miss a weekly worship experience in my church fifty-two weeks a year?"

Bible Study

Read aloud Paul's encouragement to the church in Philippians 4:4-9. Now review quickly the story of the birth of the church in Philippi from Acts 16. Remember the laywoman Lydia is likely the personal recipient of Paul's advice, and likely provides leadership in the design and implementation of worship.

Is your worship always, really and truly, *an experience of joy, felt by all the worshipers, young and old, and perceived as such by newcomers? If it is, what makes it so? If it isn't, what is lacking?*

Is your worship, and are your worship leaders, truly open to anything and everything that is honorable, just, pure, pleasing, commendable, and excellent, regardless of their personal tastes and opinions?

80

Discussion

Thriving churches rely on worship not only to teach, but also to motivate participants to go deeper into personal and spiritual growth, and to exercise their spiritual gifts and callings into mission the other six days of the week. Worship reflects "in micro" what the entire system—the thriving church—strives to achieve "in macro," namely, that people will be changed, gifted, called, equipped, and sent.

Declining churches rely on worship to entrench ecclesiastical traditions and reinforce certain social preferences for particular music, lifestyles, and ideologies. Worship reflects "in micro" what the entire system of the declining church seeks to achieve "in macro," namely, that people will be enrolled, informed, nominated, supervised, and kept.

In the thriving church, worship and organizational life are indistinguishable from each other. Organizational leaders never miss worship, and any worship participant feels he or she influences organizational decisions (regardless of this person's membership status). In the declining church, worship and organizational life are quite separate. Organizational leaders may never miss a meeting, but may be lackadaisical about worship attendance fifty-two weeks out of the year, and worship participants who are nonmembers feel powerless to influence organizational decisions. Discuss your answers to the following questions:

Why would organizational leaders ever allow themselves to miss worship?

What kind of music can best be used by the congregation to communicate joy, and by the Holy Spirit to convey hope? Is there just one kind of music that can do this?

81

What does worship directly motivate people to do immediately after church? within 24 hours? during the rest of the week?

Exercise

Discuss your answers to the following questions from the *Congregational Mission Assessment.*

What is the benefit that people receive from each worship service? (33) (NOTE: Record the average score from each worksheet on a 1-10 scale with "1" being extremely negative and "10" being extremely positive.)

Service	Personal Transformation Factor	Personal Support Factor	Motivation for Spiritual Growth Factor	Education and Learning Factor	Mission Connection Factor
#1					
#2					
#3					
#4					

How many visitors to worship came as a result of a particular mission or ministry of the church? (73)

Does worship regularly focus prayer or celebration on one or more missions or ministries that are undertaken hands-on by members in the church? (74)

82

How do we use the following public events to communicate to the public and draw them toward the church? (104)

Christmas Eve
Valentines Day
Easter
Mother's Day
Halloween
Thanksgiving

Thriving church worship is always indigenous to the surrounding community. This means that the language, music, technologies, and general format of worship are the same as are used in the everyday experience at work, home, and play of the various publics in the community.

What would your church need to change in order for worship to be indigenous to the community?

How stressful would such changes be for your church?

83

IV

TRANSFORMING THE CONGREGATION!

Read chapters 7-11 of
Kicking Habits (pages 177-234)

Yes! You can transform your congregation. There is no addict who is beyond redemption. There is no church that cannot be changed through the intervention of a Higher Power. There is no church leader who cannot be rescued, revitalized, and recommissioned through a vital connection with Jesus the Christ. There are numerous examples, of small and large, rural and urban congregations from every denomination that testify that it can be done. Indeed, many of the books and articles today read like a testimony in Alcoholics Anonymous. *We once were selfish, inward-looking churches obsessed with control and the perpetuation of a heritage, and now we are courageous, outward-looking churches devoted to volunteer empowerment and the extension of the realm of God.*

Transformation is described in *Kicking Habits* in five stages. There is not a hard and fast rule that it must come in five stages. Perhaps for your church it will be six, or seven, or maybe just one giant leap. Before looking at the process, however, we must face five of the most common misunderstandings church leaders bring to transformational change. These are the questions I hear over and over again, which reveal that the church or church leader has not really understood what this is all about.

1. How long will it take?

Whenever I hear this question, I cringe inside. Right away I know that people have missed the point. They still think that "change" has to do with "strategic planning," and have not realized that I am quite serious with the addiction metaphor. Have you ever known an alcoholic to reform as a result of strategic planning?

85

This is a process of addiction intervention and relief. Therefore, it is not a blueprint to be followed religiously by any and every congregation. The tactics for change will be customized for every context. If you approach this process as another form of strategic planning, you will miss the fundamental *attitude shift* that lies at the heart of church transformation. Your strategic planning will simply reinforce old addictive habits, because you will have failed to go deep enough to see the real problem that lies at the heart of your congregational life.

The process may well take three to five years. Perhaps more. Perhaps less. It all depends on how deeply caught in the "tornado of church decline" (see the chart earlier in this workbook) the congregation finds itself to be. However, if you are so deep into the "tornado" that you have magnetically attracted numbers of dysfunctional leaders, then you can expect in advance that these leaders will prefer strategic planning to addiction intervention.

How long will it take? It will take as long as necessary. You cannot move on to the next stage until you have generally resolved the stress of the previous stage. Some churches are more stressed in one stage, other churches more stressed in another. Everybody's addiction is different. Every church's leadership abilities are different.

2. Will we have to change everything?

Whenever I hear this question, I shake my head in sorrow. Jesus gave the answer over and over again. Indeed, it is probably his answer that got him crucified. *Of course* you have to change everything! You have to reenter the womb of God and be born again! (see John 3). You have to forsake your ancestors, and let the dead bury their own dead, and follow Jesus! (see Luke 9:60). You can't take an extra pair of shoes, a spare cloak, a bag of comfort foods, and a few million dollars in certified deposits safely on reserve in the bank with you (see Luke 10). Your world, your church, your life has got to change.

It may be that after the transformation you will still worship in the same building. It may be that you will still belong to your old denomination. It may be that the clergy will still wear cassock albs, or that the sacraments will still be served in the traditional manner. You must understand, however, that from the perspective of addiction and transformation, these things are all just tactics. The only thing that is sacred is that a congregation be willing to stake everything it is, everything it has, and everything it wants to be, in order to be with Jesus in the mission field.

It is true that this is a "both/and" world in which multiple options for a diverse public is the rule, but in order to be a "both/and" church you will have to make "either/or" choices. The "either/or" choice is to be with Jesus in the mission field. Once that choice is made, you can use as many "both/and" tactics as you wish. Addicted churches, however, espouse "both/and" jargon simply to express the age-old desire "to *have* their cake and *eat it*, too." They want to be with Jesus *and* remain content with the status quo. They want to be with Jesus *and* prioritize all their money and energy to preserve a tradition or maintain a lovely building. They want to follow Jesus to a promised land *and* keep their golden calf. True discipleship does not allow that kind of "both/and" thinking. That is idolatry. It must be shattered in order for the church to truly live. That is addiction, and as in all addiction, the first step to recovery is the hardest.

3. What must those people do first?

Whenever I hear this question, I know that the leaders are not ready for transformation. They have made some artificial distinction in their minds that separates them from the rest of the congregation. It is as if an alcoholic were to say (and they most always do say), *"Those fellows over there have a real drinking problem. How can we help them?"*

Leaders must understand from the beginning that they, too, are part of the problem. Transformation of the congregation will begin with transformation of the leader himself or herself. This is not an objectified exercise. It is intensely personal. It is very subjective. It requires leaders to face the inner dysfunctions that lie in their own hearts. It requires leaders to pluck out the logs in their own eyes, before they ever try to do surgery on the speck in their brothers' and sisters' eyes.

The real question is "What must I do first?" The story of the Philippians in Acts 16 is a wondrous analogy of church transformation. The jailer who falls at Paul's feet and asks, *"What must I do to be saved?"* is really just asking the same question as Lydia earlier in the story. The Christendom clergy are the jailers. The Christendom boards of elders are the jailers. They have helped feed the addictions of the declining church system for decades, and they need to face that responsibility. Or, to turn the metaphor around, individual church leaders must realize from the beginning that *they are all in jail together.* All share the addiction. All need the intervention of a Higher Power to shake the foundations of the prison, and set the prisoners free.

4. Can we do it quietly and without scandal?

Whenever I hear this question, I get angry. Perhaps it is because I served as a denominational leader for a number of years and grew weary of congregational leaders using the denomination as an excuse not to transform. Will it cause controversy in the judicatory? Will it jeopardize my career path? Will we fall behind in our unspoken and not-so-hidden competition with the other churches in our community?

The reality is that part of the healing process of an addict is precisely to cause a scandal. Church leaders must go public and declare their addiction. Yes, it may jeopardize your career path, although these days more and more judicatory leaders are enlightened enough to acknowledge that even the bishop is caught up in the addiction, and they are more ready than ever before to love you for your desire to break out. However, it will almost certainly compromise your supposed competitive edge with other congregations in your denomination and in your community. Other churches will, indeed, delight in pointing their fingers and saying, *"See, we told you that those people had a drinking problem!"* Let them deal with their own addiction while you get on with the process of dealing with yours.

One of the reasons you do go public is that this is the only way you can find a mutual support group. You need partners. You cannot do it alone. Once you go public, you will find other churches and church leaders, some within your denomination and some in other denominations, some within your local community and others from a different hemisphere, who can participate in the mutual mentoring that supports transformation.

5. Will this bring new people to our church?

Whenever I hear this question, I know that all the energy the church is about to pour into transformation will be a complete waste of time. These people just don't get it. They still think the object of the lesson is to cajole the public to adopt their practices and points of view, and to enlist their efforts in shouldering the burden to perpetuate their institution. People who ask this question are interested in finding a new marketing strategy to sell beer to minors that will not offend the community at large, but that will simply draw people into their circle of addiction. One way to avoid being an alcoholic is by trying to get everyone to have a drink with you.

If you follow this process of transformation, some people will leave your church. However, you will find that many others find ways to connect with your church, participate in your church, and even financially support your church. If that is how you see it, however, then you have missed the point. You remain caught in your addiction. Sooner or later the cycle of decline and death will start all over again. Why?

It is because you have misread church growth. People are not connecting with your church, but with an experience of Jesus the Christ. People are not participating in your church, but discovering the mission that is a fulfillment of their lives. People are not financially supporting your church, but contributing to an organization that helps change, gift, call, equip, and send people to be with Jesus in the mission field. And no, the two things are *not* the same.

The point of this process is not to get the public to listen to the church, but to get the church to, at long last, listen to the spiritually yearning, institutionally alienated public. Alcoholics talk too much. Haven't you noticed? They think they are experts about everything, and that their opinions matter more that those of anyone else. If you want to transform your church, shut up! Start listening! Listen to your own people. Listen to the marginal members and dropouts of the congregation. Listen to the publics who have no Christian memory. Listen to the emerging ethnic and culturally diverse communities who currently do not know, or care, that you exist. They will tell you how well you are doing in addiction recovery.

Before you begin the five-stage process of transformation (or however many stages you think it may take), I urge you to review with your church leaders the answers to these five most commonly asked questions. Then ready or not, get going!

Bible Study   Read the story of the raising of Lazarus in John 11:1-44. In a sense, the transformation you are seeking for your church is no less than a resurrection experience. It is all about being released from the tomb of your corporate addiction to live a new life that glorifies God. God says to you, "Unbind your church, and let it go free!"

a) There is both mystery and speculation about Jesus' delay and intervention.

Why is time, or timing, so important to this story?

b) The Gospel writer believes the raising of Lazarus is a crucial turning point in history.

What actually changes?

c) All of the characters in the story experience change.

Who must change the most?

d) It seems the witnesses and participants in this story are either excited or scandalized.

Could either the joy or the scandal have been managed differently?

e) Read John 12:9-11, and read about the plot to kill Lazarus.

From the vantage point of even a few years later, would Mary, Martha, and Lazarus have felt it was all worth it?

Exercise If you choose to lead transformation in your church, be prepared to answer variations on the above five questions. Discuss in your small group your answers to these questions:

1) How long will it take?

2) How much will we have to change?

3) Who will face the most change?

4) Can we avoid stress, scandal, or conflict?

5) Will it be worth it?

In *Kicking Habits,* I concentrated on explaining the goals and anticipated stress points of each stage of the process. Here, I want to concentrate on the simultaneous acts of de-construction and re-construction that will help you accomplish your goals.

91

Session 1
Build a Team Vision

Goal

In this session we will understand the need for team vision as a means to motivate all the changes to come, and how a congregation creates a climate for emerging vision.

Prayer Focus

Darken the room as much as possible. Pitch-black, inky darkness is best. Now turn on one extremely bright strobe light at a very slow speed. Focus the light on a silhouette image of a flying dove that you have posted on the wall. Try not to think. Try simply to open your mind and heart. Ask God to fly you away to where God wants you to be.

Bible Study

Read aloud the vision of John as told in Revelation 1:1-8; 21:1-7; 22:1-5. Acknowledge that these visions provide metaphors about the realm of God, and explore all of the nuances of these metaphors. Note the urgency about the coming of the realm of God, and the role that the church is supposed to play in its coming.

What is the difference between "the old" and "the new"?

Why is the description of the realm of God so filled with sensory data?

What are some of the sights, sounds, tastes, and feelings of the realm of God?

How much do you really desire, yearn, or long for the realm of God?

Discussion   The first stage of transformation is about building team visions. Discuss the ten keys to authentic, motivating visions originally found in *Kicking Habits* (page 174):

1) It's a "Song in Your Heart"
Authentic visions are not statements, essays, or understandings of the mind; each is a rhythm, beat, tune, hymn, song, verse, or lyric of the heart.

2) It makes your blood beat faster
Authentic visions do not initially make your brain work harder, but they create energy to stand, tap, act, or move. Visions create willpower. Thinking is important, but comes later.

3) It can only be communicated without words
Words will always be inadequate, and no two people will describe the vision the same way. Visions are communicated by a hug, smile, kiss, dramatic action, eye contact, and surprising intuition.

4) It is only real when shared with strangers
It is usually embarrassing to repeat it to friends, but among strangers it creates friends. Confirmation comes when the eyes of complete strangers light up in recognition.

5) It makes you feel like nobility
Authentic visions never motivate you to join an organization or be a member of a club, but they make you feel like a key part of a great destiny of personal fulfillment and universal significance.

6) It makes you want to do something—and do it now!
Authentic visions provide no patience with committees or processes of approval. They fill a person with instant eagerness and profound immediacy.

93

7) It only comes after waiting, prayer, and Bible study

Authentic visions are never planned, scheduled, or created. They are only revealed in the context of deep spirituality and dramatic change.

8) It only comes to individuals

Authentic visions never are revealed to committees, boards, or groups, but only to receptive individuals, who may not even realize how receptive they are!

9) It only survives as Team Vision

Protected by the individual it dies, but when shared and refined, the authentic vision collects and unites the people.

10) It is always "Jesus Christ"

Authentic visions convey an immediate experience of God as powerful and transforming. They connect with the second "person" of the Trinity, Jesus Christ, as the transfiguring, healing, transform-ing agent of divine will.

For an in-depth understanding of the nature, coming, and impact of biblical visions, read the vision discernment section in *Moving Off the Map* by Thomas G. Bandy (Nashville: Abingdon Press, 1998, pp. 178-99), or download the Vision Discernment resource from the *Easum, Bandy & Associates* website at *www.easumbandy.com.*

Planning   The goals for this first stage are explained in *Kicking Habits*. They are:

a) Build congregational commitment to trans-formation;
b) Create visionary, motivational congregation-al meetings;
c) Focus on discovery of spiritual gifts;
d) Flex leadership priorities.

Our focus here is on the simultaneous de-construc-tion and re-construction to accomplish these goals.

94

Remember, we are considering tactics for change, and these are highly contextual. You must feel free to customize these tactics for your situation. You may also add to the list. You can help other churches and church leaders by telling how you have added to, or customized, these tactics and sharing them with other readers by posting them on our website: *www.easumbandy.com.*

In order to make this list of tactics easier to review, I identify the more positive "re-construction" side of the activity. (Refer to *Kicking Habits*, pages 178-79.) The following tactics are not necessarily presented in order of implementation, but you will see a certain logic to the flow of events.

1. Start preaching transformation

Suspend use of the common lectionary, and preach on the great "vision" texts of the Bible. Go beyond preaching about the renewal of the church, but surrender everything to the creative genius of the Holy Spirit. You may wish to use the "Covenant of Openness" found in the vision discernment section of *Moving Off the Map,* pages 183-88. The new preaching schedule may last six to twelve months.

2. Meet in public locations

Stop holding annual meetings, board meetings, or committee meetings inside the church building. When you meet in public places (restaurants, mall food courts, sports arenas, etc.) you will find that your meeting agenda reshapes itself. Things you thought were important in the church basement become less important. Things you once barely mentioned now become the center of conversation. When you think the publics are eavesdropping on your conversation, you start listening to yourself speak. NOTE: Confidentiality may require some conversations to be held in private—but you will be forced to consider whether topics of supposed confidentiality really have to do with the hurts and needs of people, or with the desire of church leaders to save themselves from embarrassment.

3. Initiate commonsense procedure

Parliamentary procedure has become an obstacle for most people.

There are very few issues that demand *Robert's Rules of Order,* and experienced church veterans can use the rules to block others (including the Holy Spirit) from being heard. A commonsense approach is similar to the protocol for participation on many Internet services: *Be brief, be clear, and be generous to let others have their say.* That's it.

NOTE: If you live in Canada, or in a state where federal or state laws require you to file a record of your personnel and financial decisions as a charitable organization, you will still need to have accurate records of motions.

4. Redesign committees using PALS strategy

The attempt to convert traditional committees into PALS groups is not intended to always succeed. Some program committees and groups (choirs, education, generational groups) may be successfully converted, but you cannot always transform a dog into a rabbit. (See *Christian Chaos: Revolutionizing the Congregation* by Thomas G. Bandy [Abingdon Press, 1999] for a full discussion of this issue.) Your attempt to convert committees to PALS groups is intended to create stress. It forces people to begin thinking "bottom-up" rather than "top-down," and forces chairpersons to discover the different skills required to grow people rather than just administrate an agenda.

5. Maximize singing, praying, sharing

Whenever groups meet, do not allow singing and praying to become too perfunctory or liturgical. Make it more spontaneous and heartfelt. Give it more time. Enjoy it. Take more time to allow people to share the ups and downs, stresses and spiritual discoveries, of the past week. Practice what the early Methodists used to do whenever they gathered in cell groups. They asked: "How is it with thy soul?" Remember that today visions are like a song in the heart. Therefore, the more you sing, and the more variety of songs you sing, the more people attune themselves to listening to God's vision.

6. Expand mission discernment

Unless the church is in imminent danger of bankruptcy this week, most budget reviews are counterproductive. They sidetrack people from mission to survival. Therefore, take away time from budget review, and expand the time and priority given to review demographic and psychographic trends in the community, emerging regional and global mission issues, and other outreach matters. In order to make this more than just "consciousness raising," always conclude your discussion by answering two questions:

a) Is there anything our people can do about this that is "hands-on," and not just a matter of fund-raising or policy development?

b) If we were to get involved in this, exactly what would we want to do and how would we articulate our faith motivation for doing it?

7. Attach nominations to the congregation

Many declining churches appoint nominations committees from the board, and even though the open nominations to the floor of a meeting, this nominations slate usually gets elected. This encourages patronage and perpetuates control, because marginal members are rarely involved. Insist that all nominations emerge from the floor. Make sure that all people understand the challenge, gift, call, and skills needed for leadership, but do not then present a slate of officers. Let no election become automatic. Most important, if no one is nominated for an office, let the office be vacant. Never appoint anyone who is not recognized and trusted to be gifted and called to the task.

8. Commission individuals with gifts and calling

In general, you are beginning to dismantle the nominations process as the primary way laity become involved in the mission and ministry of the church. Avoid appointing people to do tasks, and concentrate on helping people fulfill their spiritual gifts and sense of calling. For some churches, this will require some education on the difference between a gift and a talent, and the difference between a sense of duty and a desire for destiny. Bring this conversation to the forefront of congregational life by making sure individuals are publicly recognized for their gifts, and commissioned through worship to exercise a calling.

9. Declare the organization to be clay

The constitution does not need to be suspended or revised. Do not fall into the trap of appointing a committee to rewrite the constitution. Just declare the constitution to be "clay," and allow leaders to shape it or mold it to creatively fit emerging circumstances. As people begin to live in PALS partnerships and discern gifts and callings, the constitution will become too rigid for effective use. Avoid appointing some sort of steering committee that will replace the constitution, because this only encourages hierarchy and control. If you must do something to reassure the anxious, begin talking about the energy field of congregational life consisting of core values and beliefs. Talk about boundaries for action, rather than requirements that must be met. As the stress of change increases, the need for clarity about boundaries in order to trust entrepreneurial leadership will become evermore clear.

10. Allow committees to experiment

Now let the committee mandates become as open to adaptation as the constitution as a whole. The same advice applies to committee work. Committees should be encouraged to establish boundaries within which individuals should be free to experiment with integrity. Be sure to help committees implement strategies to learn from inevitable mistakes. You may even model the learning process by beginning each committee meeting with the agenda item "What I did wrong this week, and what we can all learn from it."

11. Allow staff to reprioritize time

Now let the job descriptions of the staff become just as open to adaptation and experimentation. Staff, especially, may experience this flexibility as being a time management issue, rather than strictly a tasks issue. If you allow staff to reprioritize their time in the current context of change, you almost certainly find that they will spend more time in personal and professional development, in training and coaching laity, and in worship design. They will spend less time in visitation and attending administration meetings. Be sure to communicate broadly the positive reasons why this is happening.

12. Build a high-trust, high-initiative system

The multiple committees, overlapping accountability system sidetracks leadership energy toward internal liaisons and needless reporting. It also encourages competition and control. The way to encourage initiative is to eliminate the need to constantly seek permission from others to do things. This is going to increase stress around "turf protection," and probably will mean that certain activities have more than one group, while other activities go unsupported. It is an exercise in redundancy, but it is also a way of building trust. The highest trust is exercised when we allow strangers to do things in an arena that others previously controlled. Communication systems can help everyone be informed of what is happening, but without the necessity of obtaining permission.

13. Build enthusiasm for training

Enthusiasm for training requires shifts in attitude. First, volunteers need to discover the need to grow and learn in order to do well, regardless of what they are gifted and called to do. If one is gifted and called, one feels passionate about the importance of a certain activity, and therefore desirous to achieve a high standard of excellence. One *cares*. Second, program staff and lay leaders need to respond to this need for training by devoting more time to do it. They need to train others to do ministries, rather than doing it themselves. In the short term, there will be a degree of frustration here. Ministries will not be done with the quality that professional staff used to attain. In the long term, however, the lay-led ministries will be done well, and have a wider impact than those previously led by the professionals.

14. Initiate short-term learning

These changes will force the church to deemphasize large, all-inclusive groups (for "women," "men," "youth," etc.). Training and personal growth will demand smaller groups with very specific topical foci, which tend to be intensive and short term. This allows participants to move on to another group, and gradually acquire the attitudes, knowledge, or skills demanded by their gifts and callings. NOTE: You will probably be forced to increase your continuing education budget for volunteers.

15. Combine leaders and marginal members on retreat

Since biblical visions usually emerge from the edges of congregational and community life, it makes little sense to send core leaders alone on retreat. Find ways to combine core leaders and marginal members, or, better yet, the spiritually hungry and institutionally alienated public. These retreats will probably *not* take people away to the campground. They are more likely to succeed if they are held in a hotel or other environment surrounded by culture.

16. Multiply teams

Fewer and fewer people will want to invest high energy in administration when they can find more fulfillment actually doing ministry.

Eventually the nominations nightmares will cease when the church accepts the fact that it really does not need many people to do administration. However, you want to be very intentional about multiplying true teams that have the power to discern, design, implement, and evaluate mission without asking permission. For an in-depth understanding of true teams, see *Coaching Change: Breaking Down Resistance, Building Up Hope* by Thomas G. Bandy (Nashville: Abingdon Press, 2000).

17. Look for the "song in the heart"

The only mission statements that are worthwhile are born out of clarity and consensus about core values, beliefs, and vision. You are not ready to write a mission statement yet, because you are still waiting to receive the motivating vision of God for your church. Therefore, instead of sidetracking leaders into the linear and intellectual activity of writing a mission statement, guide them instead to explore songs, metaphors, images, and poetry that move their hearts. Get people talking about the metaphors or music that elicit great joy, and fill them with urgency to do great things.

18. Maximize spiritual gifts discernment

By this time, gifts discernment has gone beyond being an optional, personal exercise, and can become an intentional, corporate strategy. Designate an evening a month, or a regular schedule, for people to receive coaching for gifts discernment. Make this effort as ambitious as that of some churches that previously gave personality inventories. Personality inventories were important because they helped committees work better. Now gifts discernment is important because it helps individuals discover their mission.

19. Answer the key question

In the end, a congregation must answer the question "What is it about our experience with Jesus that this community cannot live without?" The answer begins as individual participants and leaders go deeper into themselves, their relationship with God, and their connection with mission, to answer the question for themselves. Now build every possible strategy for sharing, so that people can discuss, shape, and build these visions into a single team vision. Whether through cof-

100

fee hours or focus groups, or anything else in between, get people talking about the visions that are beginning to keep them awake at night.

Stress   *Kicking Habits* identifies the stress you can expect during this first stage of transformation. Read pages 181-85 once again. Experience from those who have used *Kicking Habits* as a guide to change reveals that the stress is what one might expect from people first confronted with their addictive habits.

1) Denial and Discomfort

The first stage of transformation brings *disharmony* to congregational life. This is why the process cannot be used as a conflict resolution process! It is best begun when the congregation experiences relative peace and stable pastoral relationships. This stage introduces a growing "chaos factor" to congregational life. It becomes more difficult to develop budgets, fill nominations vacancies, and continue routines of management and pastoral care.

You will see emerge a growing division between people who are restless, excited, and hopeful, and people who fail to see the point, worry about lost traditions, and are nostalgic about the good old days of harmony and peace. Pastors should dare to take clear, public leadership roles that share a wider vision, tempered with sympathy and understanding for those who are anxious. Lay leaders should be prepared to engage in one-to-one conversations to coach and encourage the timid.

2) Control and Fear of Change

This first stage will shake out the controllers from their hidden places in the organization. Such people will be very vocal about their opposition to the process, claiming that it is destroying the church, unfaithful to their ancestors, and a political coup by a minority led by the pastor. The personal integrity and spiritual authenticity of core leaders in the process will be challenged.

Such confrontation may be contained within the inner circles of the board, since, so far, transformation has not powerfully affected the worship services. However, this confrontation may lead to letters to the bishop, telephone campaigns against the pastor, and perhaps

101

even a vote of confidence in the leadership of the pastor or board. A pastor should prepare to model his or her spiritual disciplines clearly, and should caution his or her spouse and children of the coming stress. Lay leaders should be ready to offer personal support for the pastor and one another, and be prepared to go very public with their hopes for the future.

When stress has become relatively healthy and manageable, and when clarity about vision has begun to emerge, move on to the next stage.

Session 2
Motivate Spiritual Growth

Goal   In this session we will understand the need for adult faith formation as a means to transform the church with integrity, and how a congregation creates an environment to birth and grow spiritual leaders.

Prayer Focus   View a film borrowed from a hospital or clinic in which the birth of a healthy baby is depicted. The best video will focus on a midwife assisting a birth at home, or be an amateur video taken by a parent for the birth of his or her own child. Meditate on this film as both an emotional and a spiritual experience.

How is the film a metaphor for individual Christians giving birth to their mission or ministry?

How is the film a metaphor for a church giving birth to its mission or ministry?

Bible Study   Read aloud the message to the church of Laodicea as found in Revelation 3:14-22. Acknowledge that this message is intended to be an extended allegory to shake the church from its contentment, and motivate deeper spiritual growth and broader sacrificial mission. Explore all of the nuances of the analogy. Note the urgency about clear values and beliefs, the judgment on lukewarm contentment.

How is your church lukewarm, and what will it take to get a cauldron of spiritual growth bubbling at the heart of congregational life?

If Jesus is standing at the door of your heart, or the heart of your church, what would stop you from opening the door?

Is the purpose of the open door to let Jesus in or let you out?

Discussion   The second stage of transformation is about motivating spiritual growth, especially among adults. You may wish to review the sections on adult faith formation and worship found in *Coaching Change*.

The second stage of transformation marks a significant escalation of effort beyond the activities of leaders and core participants of the congregation. Most especially, you will be bringing significant change to worship, and this may bring deep stress to church life and the pastoral relationship of the clergy and congregation.

How can you support staff and lay leaders personally and professionally during this stage?

My book *Coaching Change* (pages 130-40) identifies five "myths of modernity" that undermine traditional worship, and which must be shattered if the congregation is to experience the full impact of the Holy. These myths are:

1) The Myth of a Controllable Holy

Deep down inside, modern church members fear the irrational and mighty power of God, and want to control or manage worship with vestments, liturgies, and pews. Members of declining churches want worship to be predictably the same every week, and look askance at emotion in the church service. *How will you shatter this myth of modernity?*

2) The Myth of Reasonable Religion

Deep down inside, modern church members want even gratuitous evil and radical grace to be explainable and understandable. They want faith to make sense, at least to the trusted professionals to whom people can refer anyone with tough questions. They want to rationalize religion, so that evil will be less painful and grace will be less shocking. *How will you shatter this myth of modernity?*

3) The Myth of Therapeutic Process

Deep down inside, modern church members like worship that calms them down, soothes their fears, and helps them adjust to the cycles of aging. Worship is an extension of pastoral care, as the church holds their hands to endure and overcome the trials of life until they die. They do not want to be troubled, challenged, or upset. *How will you shatter this myth of modernity?*

4) The Myth of Progressive Justice

Deep down inside, modern church members only want worship to motivate them to raise money for charities, administrate programs, and passively await the achievement of the just society. They do not readily connect worship and personal mission, and do not easily leave worship to engage in risky undertakings. *How will you shatter this myth of modernity?*

5) The Myth of Heavenly Favors

Deep down inside, modern church members place worship in the life context of bargaining with God. They promise to attend worship, use church envelopes, and serve the institution, in return for which God will keep them safe from harm, bless them with financial security, and provide privileges for special family celebrations regarding birth, marriage, and funerals. *How will you shatter this myth of modernity?*

For an in-depth understanding of the myths of modernity, read *Coaching Change* or visit the special web link for *Coaching Change* from the *Easum, Bandy & Associates* website: *www.easumbandy.com.*

Planning

The goals for this second stage are explained in *Kicking Habits.* They are:

a) Create a climate of expectation;
b) Involve everybody in listening for God;
c) Make worship dramatic and diverse;
d) Increase congregational communications.

Our focus here is on the simultaneous de-construction and re-construction to accomplish these goals.

Remember, we are considering tactics for change, and these are highly contextual. You must feel free to customize these tactics for your situation. You may also add to the list. You can help other churches and church leaders by sharing how you have added to, or customized, these tactics by sharing them with other readers by posting them on our website: *www.easumbandy.com.*

For further coaching about worship for the post-modern world, read the chapter on worship from *Growing Spiritual Redwoods* by William Easum and Thomas G. Bandy (Nashville: Abingdon Press, 1997).

In order to make this list of tactics easier to review, I identify the more positive "re-construction" side of the activity. (Refer to *Kicking Habits* pages 188-89). The following tactics are not necessarily presented in order of implementation, but you will see a certain logic to the flow of events.

1) Build motivational worship

Traditional worship feels more like a classroom than anything else. It is intended to educate people about the Christian year, the correct interpretation of scripture, the basic tenets of tradition, or the proper way to vote or behave. It is intended to inform people about history, coming meetings, the agenda of the institution, and personal changes among the membership. It does not motivate people to do much more than go home content to lunch, ponder theological or ethical issues, raise money, and attend meetings. Truly motivational worship, however, is encouraging, inspiring, and sends positively charged people with high emotion deeper into personal and spiritual growth to undertake hands-on missions during the week. Build worship around indigenous music and singing, sights and sounds and smells and tastes.

2) Aim for the heart

Traditional worship tends to be very wordy, rational, and intellectual. What matters is what participants think or remember following the service. Now you need to aim at the heart. What matters is how they feel. These feelings may not be always happy. Touch the deep emotions of joy and sorrow, hope and fear, victory and tragedy. Reduce the size of the bulletin, and remove any code words never used in ordinary language. Use contemporary stories and images. Tell personal stories. Move people to laughter or tears.

3) Begin a dialogue of passion

Suspend traditional expository preaching, and seek to involve the congregation in interactive dialogue. Shift from the pulpit to the main floor, and from notes to eye-to-eye contact. Invite laity from within or beyond the congregation to dialogue openly. Shorten sermons in order to make room for question-and-answer periods in worship. Establish a computer link from pew to chancel so that anonymous questions can be posed, seen, and addressed interrupting the flow of speaking. Rapid, direct, personal responsiveness to the people who are there should replace measured, objective, presentational rebuttals with people who are not in the room.

106

4) Experiment with midweek worship

Begin short-term experiments with different kinds of worship outside of the usual Sunday morning. Try healing or coaching worship services on weekday evenings. Plan extraordinary, special worship aimed at seekers for Valentine's Day, Mother's Day, Halloween, Thanksgiving, and Christmas Eve. Be sure to create new worship opportunities with teams of leaders organized as PALS groups. Do not measure success by numbers in attendance, but by how much the teams learn about the spiritual hunger of the public and the tactics that work.

5) Use everyday language and variety

Aside from the elimination of code words that only Christendom understands ("narthex," "doxology," "hymn," "anthem," etc.), the order of worship should become unpredictable. Break the repetitiveness of using the same liturgical format week after week. Rearrange the basic elements. Add and delete. Handcraft every prayer. Take nothing from a book. You know you are succeeding when people begin phoning on Saturday evening cautiously asking what Sunday morning will look like.

6) Create authenticity

Authenticity means that nothing is borrowed from any other church leader, contemporary or historical. The entire worship service, both in content and style, reflects the personal experience of the leaders. Leaders should not put on a different behavior when they lead worship, or try to live up to an abstract standard set by a seminary, or pretend to be something they are not. The words spoken in worship should be consistent with the vocabulary used in daily life. If possible, even the choral responses and the congregational leaders themselves should compose music.

7) Call for life covenants

Deemphasize the ceremony associated with financial offerings. Focus on lifetime commitments, the renewal of baptismal vows, and the surrender of the self to God's will. Aim for the spirit of the old Wesleyan Covenant: "I am no longer my own but yours. Put me to what you will, rank me with whom you will; put me to doing, put me to suffering; let me be employed for you, or laid aside for you,

107

exalted for you or brought low for you; let me be full, let me be empty; let me have all things, let me have nothing; I freely and heartily yield all things to your pleasure and disposal. And now, glorious and blessed God, Father, Son, and Holy Spirit, you are mine and I am yours. So be it. And the covenant, which we have made on earth, let it be ratified in heaven."

8) Train counselors

Since the pattern of worship is becoming unpredictable, and since worship aims at the heart, you will no longer need ushers. People need to feel free to sit anywhere, and there will be less paper to hand out. You may even begin removing some pews, or seating people around tables. You do need to train lay counselors, whose ministry will be to observe worshipers interact emotionally with the Holy, and who are trained to go to any person to offer a tissue, a prayer, a kind word, or just protect their private space. Train these people to sit long after the service is over to talk and pray with worshipers.

9) Create your own lectionary

An annual plan to share and reflect on scripture is good, but it must be your *own* plan. Do not import a common lectionary developed by strangers to your church. Let your own congregational team develop its own lectionary. Weight your lectionary heavily toward the combination of Luke-Acts.

10) Increase drama

Instead of always reading scripture, make the presentation of scripture as dramatic as possible. Use dramatic readings, chancel dramas, visual aids with photos, film clips, or computer-generated images.

11) Increase nontraditional music

Reduce the use of the organ by at least 50 percent, but do not simply turn to a grand piano. Use an electronic keyboard, woodwinds, brass, strings, and any other instrumentation imaginable. Classical music does not have to be eliminated, but it must be balanced with all other genres of music. Do dramatically reduce traditional "churchy" music. Whatever you sing, project the words on-screen and avoid traditional hymnbooks.

12) Create open space

Clear away all the clutter of furniture in the chancel rail, and reduce the presentation area to a clear stage with removable furniture. You may wish to remove the first few pews to allow even more room for music, drama, or dance. Space pews or chairs farther apart to make it easier for people to stand or move. Visually create a sense of openness and freedom.

13) Aim at intimacy

Avoid stylized invitations to "pass the peace," and surface announcements about birthdays and anniversaries. Allow multiple options for people to greet one another, and give them more time to talk and introduce themselves. Share poignant moments of joy or sorrow. Offer opportunities for personal, intercessory prayer with prayer teams following every worship service. Train key lay leaders to model risking deeper intimacy amid the congregation.

14) Aim at ecstasy

Emotion is not enough. Aim to change lives. Help people step outside themselves to escape the traps of routine. Help them to laugh at their timidity, and accept their inadequacies. Do not simply provide knowledge, however profound it might be. Do not be afraid of irrationality in worship, sudden positive or negative emotions, disruptions to orderly worship, and so on. Worship leaders should be prepared to go off on an unexpected tangent, and let go of the original plan. Music leaders especially should be prepared to take initiative, and adapt to changing circumstances.

15) Reduce policy debates

Worship committees are largely irrelevant, and only need to meet once a year (if that) to resolve any policies regarding the celebration of the sacraments peculiar to a denominational polity.

16) Create a worship design team

Create a new design team for worship planning and implementation consisting of three people. The faith sharer may be the pastor, but the role is not to reproduce a liturgy suitable for the Christian year, but to customize a message for the community context. The music coordinator may or may not be the organist, because this person should be able to utilize any and all musical genres to support the style and content of the message. The drama coach should customize worship to be interactive, and involve all the five senses. Remember: Your goal is not to create an order of service, but to create an ambience or spiritually charged atmosphere in which people will experience the Holy in often unpredictable ways.

17) Build prayer triads

Table grace should no longer be the spiritual cornerstone of congregational activities. Form triads of laity with a regular discipline to pray for the ministries and ministry leaders of the church. Some triads should pray during the actual time of each worship service, for that worship service, in an adjoining room, and the worship participants should know this. Recognize and commission these triads. Eventually, they will mentor others in spiritual growth.

18) Look to spiritual transformation

Avoid the jargon of "spiritual journeys" that never end. Focus, instead, on spiritual transformations or on the goal of new life that lies at the end of spiritual journeys. Therefore, steer people away from vague processes, and toward the concreteness of discerning spiritual gifts. Focus people on discerning how they can use their gifts to fulfill their lives.

19) Multiply communications

Eliminate verbal announcements from worship, and do not rely on physical contact to disseminate information about the church. Use new fax and Internet technologies. Multiply newsletters both in frequency and in media.

20) Multiply communicators

Eliminate the need for bulletin inserts, and use real people to communicate with newcomers. Create information booths in the vestibule, and train guides who can literally walk with people entering church for the first time.

Stress

Kicking Habits identifies the stress you can expect during this second stage of transformation. Read pages 194-99 once again. Experience from those who have used *Kicking Habits* as a guide to change reveals that the stress here is what one might expect from families trapped in codependent relationships once just one family member tries to break free.

1) Music Wars

The blur between the sacred and the profane will be felt most severely in music, as people are pushed to make a distinction between their aesthetic tastes and the mission to proclaim the gospel. Music, not doctrine, will be the center of conflict. Defenders of the organ, classical, and "churchy" traditional hymnology will criticize church leaders for "dumbing down" the faith and abandoning "good" worship. Pastors need to be prepared to talk about the difference between "taste" and "faithfulness." Lay leaders must be ready to demonstrate their own willingness to experience music that they personally dislike, for a higher goal of helping another experience the fullness of Christ.

At its most severe, organists and traditional choirs will threaten to leave the church, and may need to be fired and let go by the church. There can be no compromise. The gospel comes first. Taste and tradition come second. However, increasing numbers of music professionals may be surprisingly open and eager to experiment with all genres and instrumentations of music, or at least willing to cooperate with other music leaders who can multiply the musical options of the congregation.

Remember that music, not the spoken word, is the most potent influence today on the attitudes and lifestyles of contemporary people. That is why music is the battleground for power in the church. This battle must be won by transformational leaders for whom only the gospel matters, and everything else is tactics. You cannot move on to the next stage unless this battle is won.

2) Anxiety about the "Uncontrollable Holy"

Music wars actually do point toward another stress emerging in congregational life, namely, the irrationality or unpredictability of

111

God. Traditional church music is remarkably orderly. Its style and delivery is measured and understandable. It often soothes and calms. If it inspires, the inspiration is usually ethereal and mystical, not "down and dirty" or oriented to changed lifestyles and practical mission.

Orderly worship, and indeed, orderly congregational life, will be increasingly interrupted during this stage. Church managers will be driven to despair. People may actually be healed in worship; many will experience surges of emotion hitherto unknown. The young women will dream dreams, and the young men will think impossible things. A certain degree of "craziness" will make financial planners anxious, and alarm traditional church leaders who worry about the image of the congregation in the community. Pastors will need to loosen up and become spontaneous and adaptable. Lay leaders will begin to surrender confidence in long-range plans, and must learn how to improvise.

3) Inadequate Skills

In the first stage, leaders gleefully led the church into change, and the people reacted saying, "What have you gotten us into?" This stage will jolt leaders awake. They suddenly realize their seminary training is inadequate to church transformation. They now ask "What have I gotten myself into?"

Pastors and lay leaders will need to trust their instincts more than their traditional training. They will need to find mentors, form partnerships, and go out and learn from other churches experiencing transformation.

The stress in this stage will never entirely go away. However, when it does become relatively healthy, and when leaders have survived the ensuing conflicts to intuitively believe that the church will be "OK," you can move on to the next stage. Indeed, you will earnestly desire to press on because leaders will recognize that only then will some of the tension and anxiety be relieved. You are ready to move on when the congregation recognizes that *there is no going back now!*

Session 3
Free Leaders to Lead

Goal

In this session we will understand the nature of strong pastoral and lay leadership for change, and begin to discern the attitudes and skills necessary to lead transformation.

Prayer Focus

Obtain a sound effects recording of a thunderstorm. Darken the room as much as possible and play the recording at a high volume. Alternatively, obtain a film clip of a huge wave overpowering a ship from the classic movies *The Poseidon Adventure* or *The Perfect Storm,* and show them to the group. Imagine living in the chaos of the storm. Feel the rush of adrenaline. Sense the mystery about what the outcome of the storm might be. Meditate on these questions:

If I were leading my family or a group of people in the midst of such a storm, how would I need to behave?

If I were experiencing such a storm, where would I find the courage to lead?

Bible Study

Read aloud the story of Paul's shipwreck in Acts 27:1-44. Aside from being a good story that legitimizes Paul's claim to apostleship, the story is included in the Bible as an analogy of the church enduring and overcoming the tribulations of life. Reflect on the nature of leadership in the midst of the storm.

How do others treat the leader before, during, and after the storm? How do people distort the realities of leadership? How do people recognize authentic leadership?

113

How does a leader understand himself or herself in the midst of the storm? How is this different from the way a leader behaves in calmer times?

How do you be hopeful in the midst of a huge storm?

Discussion

The third stage of transformation is about redefining leadership roles. You may wish to review the section describing spiritual leadership that is visionary, disciplined, and courageous found in *Coaching Change*.

The third stage of transformation shifts the focus from the congregation to the leaders themselves. Notice that this does not precede, but follows, the chaos of change precipitated by deepening spirituality. Leaders cannot anticipate change, and then lead it. First they experience chaos, allow it to test them, and then learn from within the midst of stress. Theory does not precede application. Chaos gives birth to innovation.

In *Growing Spiritual Redwoods*, transformational leaders are described in three ways. You may wish to review the appropriate chapter in this book.

1) Visionary

Visionary leadership sees the goal of true discipleship that lies beyond the institutional church. Visionary leaders sense the nearness of land, and the presence of a safe haven, even when their senses are limited by the fury of the storm.

Who are the visionary leaders in our congregation, and how can we support them?

2) Synthesizer

Synthesizing leadership brings together disparate, even opposite things to create something fresh and new. Synthesizing leaders build bridges between personalities, forge new partnerships within and beyond the church, and bring together seemingly polar opposites in common ground. They scramble to find a way to triumph over the storm.

Who are the synthesizing leaders in our congregation, and how can we support them?

3) Midwife
Midwifing leadership helps individuals give birth to the potentialities that God has implanted in every human being. Midwifing leaders passionately persuade or challenge others to give birth, and raise up, the mission-child that is within them.

Who are the midwives in our congregation, and how can we support them?

These metaphors are further elaborated in *Leadership on the OtherSide* by Bill Easum (Nashville: Abingdon Press, 2000). This is one of the best books available to understand what it is like to be a leader in the midst of sweeping religious and cultural change.

Planning

The goals for this third stage are explained in *Kicking Habits*. They are:

a) *Shift clergy from "enabling" to "training";*
b) *Shift lay leadership from "managing" to "futuring";*
c) *Shift lay participation from "fund-raising" to "ministry";*
d) *Insist on quality.*

Our focus here is on the simultaneous de-construction and re-construction to accomplish these goals.

Remember, we are considering tactics for change, and these are highly contextual. You must feel free to customize these tactics for your situation. You may also add to the list. You can help

115

other churches and church leaders by sharing how you have added to, or customized, these tactics and sharing them with other readers by posting them on our website: *www.easumbandy.com.*

In order to make this list of tactics easier to review, I identify the more positive "re-construction" side of the activity. Refer to *Kicking Habits* (pages 201-2). The following tactics are not necessarily presented in order of implementation, but you will see a certain logic to the flow of events.

1) Develop proscriptive mandates

Traditional committee mandates are task lists that tell people what they must do. Turn these upside down by developing mandates that simply identify what committees may *not* do ("proscriptive"). See *Christian Chaos* for a complete description and examples.

2) Initiate policy governance

Traditional organizations require all management decisions to be approved by a board or executive. Remove the management role, and concentrate only on the development of foundational governance policies. So long as policies are followed, board and executives need not review management decisions at all. This frees lay leadership from tactical discussions. (See *Christian Chaos,* pages 41-61.)

3) Focus a visionary board

If tactical decisions are removed from the board agenda, it becomes unnecessary for the board to review financial statements. Now the board can focus on the long-term future of the church. Board members can review demographic trends, dialogue with community leaders, pray for spiritual guidance, and concentrate on vision. (See *Christian Chaos* for examples of future board agendas).

4) Listen to the community

Deploy lay leaders in triads to listen to the unchurched public, observe their behavior, interpret emerging needs, and consider how the church can relevantly address public yearning with the gospel. This should occupy at least half of the time of the board leadership.

5) Train intensively

Declining churches accept volunteers without further training, and this practice must end. It encourages mediocrity, and since most people want to take pride in their work it ultimately discourages volunteerism. Training time and strategy will vary according to the position. Rely on laity to train apprentices, shift staff from doing ministries to training ministers, and don't be afraid to use the continuing education budget to send laity beyond the church for training.

6) Emphasize relational skills

Whatever the task involved, it is the relational skills that are the most important. These skills include listening, team participation, cooperation, communication, and conflict resolution.

7) Celebrate lay ministry

Celebrate the changing roles of clergy and laity in worship. Trained lay ministers should be commissioned by laying on of hands and prayer. Include volunteers doing even the "lowliest" of tasks. Laity and clergy should always share worship leadership. Newsletters should be filled with stories of lay ministries.

8) Deploy lay visitation

The most urgently needed trained lay teams to deploy are for routine visits to homes, rapid visits to newcomers, and post-funeral and post-hospitalization visits. This will not only free clergy for their emerging role as trainers and coaches, but it will more rapidly disseminate the emerging vision of the church and assist members to celebrate change.

9) Deploy clergy among the unchurched

Just as board members need to listen to the unchurched, so also clergy must spend more time among nonmembers. In addition to listening and observing, they should engage in active dialogue as much as possible. Remember, the dialogue should be mutually respectful. Clergy are not among the public to teach, so much as to learn. Discover the nuances of spiritual hunger and institutional alienation for age, gender, economic background, and ethnic status.

10) Refer long-term counseling

Pastors should begin referring any counseling relationship that appears to require more than three sessions. Long-term counseling will reduce the effective leadership of the pastor, and allow a handful of dysfunctional people to occupy most of his or her time. Refer them to other capable counselors.

11) Find cell-group shepherds

In preparation for multiplying cell groups in the future, start finding and training cell-group shepherds. If you use spiritual gifts inventories, look for people with gifts in hospitality, faith sharing, or relationship building (counseling, mentoring, etc.). Otherwise, share the profile of small-group leadership such as the one found in *Christian Chaos* (pages 234-37), and ask worshipers to submit three names that come to mind. Collate the names, and see which ones surface most often. Visit, invite, and train these people.

12) Increase personnel support

Declining churches only use personnel committees intermittently for crisis intervention, complaint management, or salary discussion. Thriving churches encourage personnel committees to meet regularly to focus on prayer and personal support for the pastor and his or her family and for other staff and their families, and to develop strategies to enhance the credibility and authenticity of staff.

13) Do performance reviews for lay leaders

Broaden the role of the personnel committee to do performance reviews of lay leaders. This will enhance and encourage their training, raise their self-esteem, and build respect for them in the church. Remember, this is a *positive* and *regular* task, not to be confused with conflict resolution or crisis intervention. The three questions to ask are: *1) Have you gone beyond the energy field of our core values, beliefs, or vision? 2) Have you done anything the proscriptive mandate expressly said that you could not do?* and *3) How can we help you continue to improve your skills?*

14) Develop an attitude of responsibility for pastoral care

Declining church members believe that "pastoral care" is not their job, it's what they pay the clergy to do. Change this attitude

118

through preaching, storytelling by laity, apprenticing laity to accompany clergy, and any other means possible. Reserve clergy caregiving solely for intensive-care hospital visits, and for those few elderly who insist that only a visit from the clergy will do.

15) Create caregiving teams

The next set of lay teams to deploy will be visitors to hospitals and nursing homes. Train them well, multiply positive stories of their work, and build increasing credibility. This will not only free the clergy for their emerging training role, but in the end the laity will do more and better quality caregiving.

16) Mentor the trusted few

Clergy dramatically reduce one-to-one, room-to-room, house-to-house visitation. Handpick a few core leaders (from among core participants and marginal members) who intuitively understand and model the core values, beliefs, and vision of the congregation, and who are eager to follow Jesus into the future mission field. Spend time sharing, mentoring, praying, and generally supporting one another. Equip them to be spiritual guides for the church.

17) Increase continuing education budgets

As volunteerism and training demands increase, so also increase continuing education budgets for laity.

18) Learn from other churches

Send teams of observers to spend time with thriving congregations, talk with their staff and leaders, understand their attitudes toward mission, and consider how to customize their strategies for your unique identity and context.

19) Build partnerships

Seek out congregations within and beyond your judicatory and denomination—regionally and globally—with whom you can trade insights, share coaching, and share resources. Also look for agencies, parachurch organizations, nonprofit organizations, and other bodies that can help train your volunteers or partner in accomplishing emerging missions.

20) Accelerate gifts discernment

As interest in the ministries of your church quickens among people within the church and the general public, increase emphasis on gifts discernment. Draw people into the cycle of being changed by the Holy, growing to discern spiritual gifts, being trained to use gifts in response to call, and being sent in teams to do beneficial services and share faith.

Stress

Kicking Habits identifies the stress you can expect during this third stage of transformation. Read pages 208-12 once again. Experience from those who have used *Kicking Habits* as a guide to change reveals that the stress here is what one might expect from addicts who simultaneously refuse to take responsibility for themselves and demand authority over the lives of others.

1) Obsession that only clergy can be caregivers

This obsession will emerge from both laity and clergy, because you are shattering a traditional codependence that has existed for centuries in the modern era. Laity find it hard to believe that other laity can provide caregiving with the same sacramental depth, confidentiality, and skill, which they presume the clergy to possess. Constant training and very public storytelling will slowly build credibility for lay leaders gifted and called in these ministries. Clergy, on the other hand, will feel enormous guilt that they are not personally visiting everyone. Apprenticing relationships with laity, support groups, and renewed spiritual disciplines that include prayer, Bible study, and reading about the earliest apostolic church will build self-esteem around a new model of ministry.

This same obsessive codependency extends to worship responsibilities (especially regarding the sacraments), institutional management, and social justice advocacy. Even the best intentioned laity and clergy will fall prey to the addiction to clergy dominance in these areas. It is truly an *addiction*, to which clergy and laity will return as soon as they relax their self-discipline. You may wish to develop mutual support groups that may even resemble 12-step programs in which clergy and laity can support one another. Read the leadership chapter in *Moving Off the Map*, pages 15-40.

2) Anxiety that things might get out of control

A parallel addiction to hierarchy or bureaucracy induces a constant, vague anxiety among church leaders during this stage. It is not that anything *in particular* is going wrong, but rather the fear that something *might* go wrong. Clergy and laity may leap at trivialities, or exaggerate small mistakes, or even manufacture imagined errors, in order to legitimize their anxiety. It is similar to the withdrawal symptoms of substance abusers known as "the shakes." The temptation will be very strong to appoint ad hoc committees, increase supervision, or require more internal reporting. Resist it!

Instead, reassure leaders by building constant clarity about the core values, beliefs, and vision that is the "energy field" of congregational life. Make this a primary accountability vehicle for the church. It functions as a boundary beyond which creativity cannot go, and brings balance to the seeming chaos that is emerging in congregational life.

Much of this anxiety for North Americans is due to a misplaced confidence in strategic planning. In the declining church system, mission emerged from the bureaucratic process of five- to ten-year planning by a central administration. As the thriving church system is established, mission will emerge only from the spiritual growth of the people. See the section on "Ministry Mapping" in *Moving Off the Map*, pages 239-78.

3) Unwillingness by adults to undertake personal or spiritual growth

The most powerful addiction that is being shattered at this stage is the belief that the youth (children, Sunday school, etc.) are the future of the church. Declining church members resist the urgent demand of God to grow. They do not feel the need. They want to escape responsibility for personal and spiritual growth by imposing it on the youth, or on the staff. Core lay leaders must be prepared to publicly share their own spiritual growth disciplines, and sing the glories of adult faith formation.

For a deeper understanding of adult faith formation in the postmodern world, see *Coaching Change*. The key strategies to motivate adults for spiritual growth are:

121

a) Multiply options by offering as many curriculums, methods, or partners as possible so that adults can choose a process that best suits their needs;

b) Orient spiritual growth to lifestyle rather than meetings, so that adults "do it" in the context of daily living and do not have to "make time" for it;

c) Always build covenant partnerships of three or four adults so that they can mutually support one another in spiritual growth, just as they diet, exercise, and jog in a group.

The stress uncovered in this stage can be managed, but it will not disappear. The addictions that cause the stress will reappear as soon as leaders relax their self-discipline, just like alcoholics slip back into substance abuse the minute they convince themselves they are "cured." Fortunately, the spiritually yearning and institutionally alienated publics are far more familiar with personal growth processes than are traditional church members. As they become attracted to the church, the pressure of their enthusiasm for personal and spiritual growth, and for personal fulfillment through mission, will positively build energy for adult faith formation. Therefore, once you get the monolithic boulder rolling, it will gain momentum.

Session 4
Streamline the Organization

Goal

In this session we will understand the need to streamline the organizational structure and learn to maintain momentum for change by embedding core processes into the system.

Prayer Focus

Place a potted plant on a table in the center of the room. Your goal is to water the plant. The plant is the spiritually thirsty public, the water is the gospel, and you are a traditional church organization.

a) Send three people to the kitchen to obtain a pitcher, and bring it back.

b) Send three different people to find a pot, fill it with water, and return.

122

c) Now appoint two more people to carefully pour the water from the pot into the pitcher.

d) Send one person to find a cloth to wipe up the spills, while the others wait.

e) Appoint a different person to wipe the spill with the cloth provided.

f) Appoint yet another person to examine the floor to make sure no drips have been missed.

g) Ask the remaining people to elect someone to actually carry the pitcher of water and set it on the table beside the plant.

h) Now ask the entire group to discuss who among them is the most holy so that they can be entrusted to actually pour the water from the pitcher onto the plant.

i) Send that holy person to water the plant.

j) Select three people to review the process, identify a mistake, and make a complaint.

k) Appoint another person to be the bishop who reviews the complaint and requests that the process be done over again for the sake of harmony in the church.

l) Send three people to the kitchen to obtain a different pitcher, and bring it back, and start the whole process over again.

m) Repeat until people become bored and threaten to go home.

Meditate on the process silently, and reflect on these questions:

Were you bored?
Were you frustrated?
Were you honored to be chosen as the most holy of the group?
Were you jealous of the person chosen to be most holy in the group?
Would you be willing to do this every time a plant needed to be watered?

Do you feel any guilt regarding the fact that you have entirely forgotten the thirsty plant?

Bible Study

Read aloud Paul's admonition to the Corinthian church in 1 Corinthians 3:1-15, 21-23. The Corinthian church was an unruly yet creative community of believers. The organizational solution to disorder, however, was neither hierarchy nor bureaucracy. It was clarity about the equal partnership they shared to accomplish a single purpose.

Every human being is gifted. Every Christian is called. Every disciple will be tested. The measure of success is growth. This means growth as individuals and as a Body of Christ. It also means expansion of God's realm and the fulfillment of God's purposes in the world. Discuss your answers to these questions:

Am I growing to understand my potential for God's mission in the world?

Is our congregation growing to mirror the demographic diversity of our community?

What percent of our combined energy is brought consciously and directly to bear on the mission field beyond the church?

Discussion

The fourth stage of transformation is about streamlining organization. You may wish to read *Christian Chaos*. Read the second half of that book first, because it describes the actual experience of empowering laity and multiplying cell groups. Then read the first half, which articulates in detail the theory of the servant-empowering organization.

The fourth stage of transformation shifts the focus from leadership development to organizational structures. Notice that this does not precede, but follows, the chaos of change precipitated by deepening spirituality and changing leadership roles. Organizational change never precipitates systemic change, but systemic change brings on a chaos that eventually demands new organizational structures.

The servant-empowering organization requires three things that are usually missing in traditional church structures.

1) A profound emphasis on individual and partnered adult spiritual growth.

Since all missions will emerge from the spiritual growth and discernment of the people, rather than be received by judicious commands of a hierarchy, there must be broad enthusiasm for adult faith formation.

> *Does our congregation now experience broad enthusiasm for adult spiritual growth that will allow us to create a servant-empowering organization?*

2) Clarity and consensus about the "genetic code" of congregational life.

The "genetic code" is another way of describing the "energy field" discussed in *Kicking Habits*. It is the shared, transparent understanding of the congregation about core values, bedrock beliefs, motivating vision, and key mission that are the boundaries beyond which creativity cannot go, but within which people are free to experiment as they wish. The "genetic code" metaphor, however, emphasizes how this clear consensus is embedded in every person and ministry of the Body of Christ.

> *Do we have such broad clarity and consensus that we can use them as the chief accountability vehicles of the servant-empowering organization?*

125

3) Intentional multiplication of true teams.

True teams have the power to discern, design, implement, and evaluate mission without having to consult with, or obtain permission from, a board. They are entrepreneurial units that are trusted because the genetic code has been embedded within them.

> *Do we understand the nature of true teams, and are we successfully beginning to deploy them for visitation, caregiving, and other missions?*

If the answer is "no" to any of the above questions, delay your progress to this fourth stage of transformation, or expect that the completion of this fourth stage will require more time, and may involve additional stress.

Although the five stages in *Kicking Habits* are presented in a linear fashion and sound very orderly and logical, the actual experience of transformation is very messy. It is not uncommon at this point to discover that you must revisit the first three stages once again to further refine your change process. Now is a good time to look back, reinforce learning, and check stress levels among leaders and participants.

Planning   The goals for this fourth stage are explained in *Kicking Habits* (page 213). They are:

> *a) Establish the "energy field" of vision, beliefs, and values;*
> *b) Create the "stability triangle" for management;*
> *c) Shift program development to cell groups;*
> *d) Multiply entry points into congregational life.*

Our focus here is on the simultaneous de-construction and re-construction to accomplish these goals.

Remember, we are considering tactics for change, and these are highly contextual. You must feel free to customize these tactics for your situation. You may also add to the list. You can help other churches and church leaders by telling how you have added to, or customized, these tactics and sharing them with other readers by posting them on our website: *www.easumbandy.com.*

In order to make this list of tactics easier to review, I identify the more positive "re-construction" side of the activity. Refer to *Kicking Habits* (pages 213-14). The following tactics are not necessarily presented in order of implementation, but you will see certain logic to the flow of events.

1) Identify and celebrate the "energy field"

This fundamental identity of shared values, beliefs, vision, and mission should be celebrated in every annual meeting, recognized regularly in worship, and communicated to all newcomers. It should also be the first thing taught new leaders, cell groups, staff, and new members. Remember: It is the primary vehicle of accountability that replaces supervision.

2) Increase singing "the song in the heart"

Biblical visions are images, metaphors, or songs that elicit incredible joy and urgently demand to be shared with strangers. The congregational vision should be seen or sung in every worship experience.

3) Match committee activity to public need

If you must have a committee, make sure that it arises in response to a clearly definable public need, rather than an internal institutional need. In the interim period while you are building wide ownership for adult spiritual growth, such committees may yet be needed to address urgent gaps in mission. Once enthusiasm for spiritual growth becomes widely shared, such committees will be replaced by true teams.

4) Discern those with the gift of administration

You will still need a small team of people to administer the resources of the church so that they can be used to deploy gifted, called ministers and mission teams. Make sure that persons nominated or appointed have the spiritual gift of administration, feel called to the work as a ministry, and are willing to be trained. Otherwise, don't let them serve in administration regardless of their skills or business background.

127

5) Create a "human resources team"

The mission of the human resources team is to grow Christians, and therefore ministers, and therefore leaders. This team will now replace the old personnel committee with a wider mandate to help both staff and volunteers grow in awareness of gifts and callings, and become equipped for ministries of excellence. (See pages 81-83 and 126-27 of *Christian Chaos* for an in-depth discussion of the mandate of this team.)

6) Make it easier to get involved

Make it easier for newcomers to participate in the church. On the one hand, eliminate the need to acquire specialized knowledge to understand worship, engage in mission, or otherwise participate in church life. On the other hand, multiply the ways people can connect with the church by means of worship, cell groups, mentors, missions, websites, and so forth. Make sure that every entry point into the church is well marked with the identity of core values, beliefs, vision, and mission, but does not try to recruit anyone into institutional service.

7) Emphasize participation over membership

Stop worrying about maintaining inactive or nonresident membership lists. Insofar as your denominational polity will allow, detach the meaning of membership from privileges, entitlements, voting power, or office holding. Privileges and entitlements should extend to guests, not members. Voting power and office holding should be given participants who are there and engaged. Connect membership solely with a "covenant to go deep" into oneself, healthy relationships, and God.

8) Appoint only gifted and called volunteers

As you transition to a new organizational model, accept unfilled gaps in the old nominations process. These will increase, but no longer because of lay leadership burnout. First, most offices and committees will become unnecessary as gifts discernment and team building gather momentum. Ministries will be done faster and more efficiently without these offices and committees than with them. Second, more and more veteran church members will opt out of committees in favor of true teams, because the latter offer more room for creativity and hope for fulfillment. In other words, nominations gaps at this stage do not just mean rejection of an old organizational model, but the positive preference for the new one.

9) Focus board agendas on "futuring"

Continue the process begun in the previous stage, eliminating entirely finance and property matters from the board agenda. Focus board members exclusively on discerning the long-term future of the congregation. Remember, this is not a strategic planning role. It is a commitment to listen to the community, observe the mission field, and hear God's call. It is more purely *spiritual leadership*.

10) Create an "administration team"

The process of delegating administration (financial and property management, trusteeship, program coordination, and communication) begun in the previous stage should now become formalized. The human resources team will begin to identify those with gifts and calling in administration. Create the administration team to be a "trusted, gifted few" to whom is delegated the management of the church. These may be elected in classes or appointed, as polity and state or provincial laws may require. The important thing is that they are given a *proscriptive* mandate that you began writing in the previous stage. (See pages 70-81 of *Christian Chaos* for an in-depth discussion of this mandate.)

11) Focus stewardship on resourcing

As more and more mission emerges from the spiritual growth of the people, and as proscriptive thinking automatically assumes permission to experiment within boundaries of clear consensus, stewardship becomes a matter of resourcing ministries rather than maintaining programs. Multiply options for giving, and surrender a unified budget. Mission teams will begin raising their own money for their own needs.

12) Emphasize public communication over internal liaisons

Continue the process of multiplying communication options begun in stage 2. Dramatically reduce the number of interoffice memos, reports, and internal liaisons, and design all communications for public view. Such transparency will build credibility in the community. Since true teams are entrepreneurial units, redundancy

129

is no longer feared. Communicating the details of management is less important, but communicating the mission goals and the identity of the congregation shaped around core values, beliefs, and vision is everything.

13) Reorient annual congregational meetings

Annual meeting should never do management. The only function of an annual meeting is to define, refine, and celebrate the "energy field" or "genetic code" of congregational life. The congregation as a whole must take ownership of the core values, beliefs, vision, and mission of the local church. (See pages 120-26 of *Christian Chaos* for an in-depth discussion of the annual meeting agenda.)

14) Aim at full disclosure of important information

Provide members and participants with all the relevant facts regarding the mission of the human resources team administration team as they grow Christians and deploy ministries. Hold nothing back that is important, and do not rely on ad hoc committees to filter information.

15) Multiply mission teams

In previous stages you began building teams for worship, visitation, and caregiving. Now multiply teams to do all programs, tasks, or ministries in the church. Never deploy anyone alone. Always deploy a team to get anything done. Remember: the team leaders will not emerge from nominations processes, but from the ferment of adult faith formation in the congregation. The rule of thumb is: *No ministry without a team—no team without a ministry.*

16) Write proscriptive mandates and job descriptions

Empower the mission goal of every team with a proscriptive job description. Such a job description does not tell the team what to do, but simply identifies boundaries beyond which they cannot go or executive limitations on their actions. Rewrite every job description in the same fashion, including that of the pastor. (See pages 98-117 of *Christian Chaos* for an in-depth discussion of these job descriptions.)

17) Design and implement all programs through PALS group process

Convert any existing program or generational groups (including Sunday school teachers, women's groups, men's groups, youth groups, etc.) to the PALS group process. Decentralize large groups into confederations of smaller cell groups.

18) Recognize and celebrate only those missions that emerge "from below"

Establish and communicate publicly the "bottom-up" nature of the new organization that only implements mission as it emerges from the spiritual growth of the participants, and never implements mission that is simply passed down from a hierarchy or imposed by outside forces.

19) Rename the church

Change the name of the church to reflect the motivating vision of the congregation. Avoid historical names unless they refer to the first apostolic age. Shun geographic names unless they clearly communicate a mission context for the church. Eliminate or deemphasize the denominational identity of the congregation.

20) Create a "training team"

Establish and communicate publicly the core process of the congregation. Abandon or deemphasize the liturgical year, and concentrate on the core process to change, gift, call, equip, and send people to be with Jesus in the mission field.

Stress

Kicking Habits identifies the stress you can expect during this fourth stage of transformation. Read pages 219-21 once again. Experience from those who have used *Kicking Habits* as a guide to change reveals that the stress here is what one might expect from addicts who both arrogantly insist they can "do it alone," but also erroneously believe that no one else can do anything without them.

1) Resistance to partnerships

Cellular organizations need to be sensitive to the great diversity of personality types, but trained cell-group leaders can adjust the relationship-building and faith-building flows of cell-group experience to nurture all kinds of people. The deeper resistance to team ministry comes from the extreme autonomy of American society. The rugged individualism that once made America great cannot survive the experience of blur, flux, and speed typical of the postmodern world. (See *Leadership on the OtherSide*.) The need to form partnerships, and the demand to surrender a measure of autonomy for the sake of team mission, is an affront to many baby boomers of the "me" generation.

Initially, the servant-empowering organization attracts those who seek personal fulfillment through the discernment of personal gifts and callings. It is when the church insists that equipping and sending individuals *in teams* is the best way to do mission that these same individualists resist the new organizational model.

Staff need to conscientiously model team leadership so that laity can understand and appreciate the efficacy of team mission. Lay leaders need to coach church veterans to understand the quantum difference in speed and complexity of the postmodern world. The organization as a whole must stand firm in its insistence to deploy only teams, and it can legitimize its decision by comparative storytelling that contrasts the accomplishments of one against the accomplishments of teams.

2) Misplaced demands for consensus

An attitude shift lies behind much of the tactical change of this stage. The order of transformation is to start with behavioral modification, and allow that to create a positive stressful environment that eventually leads people to recognize and change their underlying attitude. Once the attitude begins to shift, the stress of behavior modification disappears. Therefore, there is a psychological barrier that needs to be overcome. The attitude shift is to perceive that the congregation is building a consensus of the *heart*, rather than a consensus of the *mind*.

Traditional organizations have assumed that church unity depends on *agreement*. People must agree about every decision, program, and plan. This leads traditional organizations into *consensus management*. If an annual meeting is not doing *management*, then consensus is not being achieved.

132

Servant-empowering organizations assume that church unity depends on *shared experience*. It is not a rational agreement, so much as an irrational disposition to trust. Therefore, consensus is built around clarity about the "energy field" or "genetic code" of core values, beliefs, vision, and mission. Annual meetings do not do management, but define, refine, and celebrate that "energy field."

It is not uncommon for congregations to revisit their consensus about the "energy field" during this stage. This is because the multiplying mission teams will constantly test the boundaries of congregational life by their incredible creativity and enthusiasm. They push refinements to the shared experience of values, beliefs, and vision that the congregation previously had not imagined.

3) Mistimed denominational loyalty

Denominational loyalty is not so much misplaced, as it is mistimed. The experience of speed, blur, and flux in the postmodern world has rendered denominational hierarchies and representative bureaucracies obsolete. The same phenomenon is true for all secular organizations as well. The problem with denominational loyalty is not that it is wrong, but only that it doesn't work if your goal is to maximize mission today.

The moment the emerging servant-empowering organization announces that only those missions that emerge from the spiritual growth of the participants will be implemented, it will be criticized by judicatory leaders and church veterans who rely on the hierarchy to tell them what missions to do. This will be perceived by some as a rejection of denominational authority.

Church leaders will need to coach both judicatory leaders and veteran church members to see that denominational partnerships are not necessarily being broken, only reshaped. The link between congregation and denomination does not depend on hierarchy, but itself becomes a team relationship. Denominations now partner with congregations by supporting adult faith formation and pooling capital resources to equip continuing education and emerging mission, *but they no longer tell congregations what missions must be done.* Seen in this light, servant-empowering congregations do not have to be "disloyal" to the denomination. They are redefining their relationship to the denomination.

133

The common experience of congregations in transformation is that sometime during this stage they turn the corner or experience a breakthrough, and stress is dramatically reduced. This may be the result of some people leaving the church who are either so addicted to control, or so far alienated from the "energy field" of church life, that they cannot remain. It may also be the result of the influx of new people who start coming to the changing church, and their experiences at work, home, and play with the postmodern world as well as new organizational models building tolerance for experimentation and risk. Primarily, however, the breakthrough occurs because more and more well-meaning church veterans finally begin to experience a fundamental shift of heart. Behavior modification has finally shifted their attitudes.

Session 5
Birth a New System

Goal

In this session we will discern the fullness of the core process to change, gift, call, equip, and send people, and understand the strategy of multiplying options.

Prayer Focus

Here are two alternatives among many to focus your prayers. If you can be outdoors, purchase several cases of bottled or canned soda pop. Shake thoroughly. Give everybody a bottle or can. Face each other. On the count of three, point them at each other, open them, and have fun.

If you are indoors, give every person a balloon. Blow them up. Arm yourselves with pen or pencil. On the count of three, burst the balloons and listen to the crescendo of noise that fills the room.

Reflect on the chaos, the fun, and the mess, and consider what it means to be in mission in a world of speed, blur, and flux.

Consider what other exercises could make a similar point among different kinds of people.

Pray for all the gifts and missions that God can let loose from your people, which can affect the world in unimaginable ways.

Bible Study   Read aloud Paul's famous words in Philippians 3:7-16. Reflect on the metaphor of the race, not as a competition, but as an expression of urgency. Notice the clear focus on Christ alone, and remember how you answered the key question, "What is it about my experience with Jesus that this community cannot live without?" Notice the sense of incompletion, and the spirit of eager anticipation, communicated in Paul's words.

In your own words, what exactly is the goal toward which you are running?

What have you attained so far?

What lies ahead?

Discussion   The fifth stage of transformation is about birthing the new system. (You may wish to read the section on "Ministry Mapping" found in *Moving Off the Map*, pages 239-78). This stage of transformation marks the completion of a transformational process that may have taken three to seven years to complete. It also marks the beginning of a whole new process of exploration and mission in the postmodern world.

135

"Ministry Mapping" is the postmodern alternative to traditional strategic planning. It does not predict milestones for a world that is consistent and predictable. Instead, it poises the congregation to seize emerging opportunities in a chaos of cultures. Discuss the keys to "Ministry Mapping":

1) Mission arises from spiritual formation

The thriving church system does not rely on the brainstorming of the board, but on the spiritual growth of participants, to discern future mission. This has enormous implications. This means that church leaders cannot predict future mission. All they can do is embed a core identity, nurture personal, relational, and spiritual growth, prepare capital pools of support, train and coach whatever skills become necessary, and get out of the way.

How comfortable are you in relying on the spiritual growth of participants to shape the future of congregational mission?

2) Accept the reality of gaps in ministry

Thriving churches never have all the bases covered. They are always scrambling. They are always living on the financial edge. Yet they must exercise enormous patience and spiritual discipline, allowing mission to emerge in God's own time. They do not respond to the denomination's agenda, the community's agenda, or the world's agenda. They respond only to God's agenda.

How comfortable are you in living at the edge of your financial reserves?

3) Celebrate redundancy

Thriving churches believe in the heart that the only thing sacred is the gospel; everything else is tactics. There is no "turf protection." More than one group can address the same issue simultaneously. More than one strategy will work. More than one public has a

136

unique spiritual need. More than one person has a good perspective on the truth. A radical pragmatism dominates the congregation. They do whatever works. They become all things to all people, that by all means some might be saved.

> *How comfortable are you in allowing others to work independently in your corner of the mission field?*

4) Expect some failure and plan to learn from it

Thriving churches reward experimentation. They value mistakes as opportunities to learn. They plan in advance for inevitable failures. Their clarity and consensus about core values, beliefs, vision, and mission provide them with criteria to evaluate results. Thriving churches do mission without safety nets, in the sense that they take responsibility for success or failure and do not rely on denominations to subsidize their ministries.

> *How comfortable are you doing mission without safety nets?*

Planning

The goals for this fifth stage are explained on page 224 of *Kicking Habits*. They are:

a) Regular multi-track worship;
b) Visionary, motivating leadership;
c) Diversified and equipped discipleship;
d) Unity of faith-sharing and social action

Our focus here is on the simultaneous de-construction and re-construction to accomplish these goals.

Remember, we are considering tactics for change, and these are highly contextual. You must feel free to customize these tactics for your situation. You may also add to the list. You can help other churches and church leaders by telling how you have added to, or customized, these tactics and sharing them with other readers by posting them on our website: *www.easumbandy.com.*

In order to make this list of tactics easier to review, I identify the more positive "re-construction" side of the activity. Refer to pages 224-25 of *Kicking Habits.* The following tactics are not necessarily presented in order of implementation, but you will see certain logic to the flow of events. Many of the tactics of the fifth stage confirm and develop the initiatives of earlier stages.

1) Define identity by vision, values, and beliefs

Recognize that the congregation is now a new creation. It is not that you reject or devalue the past, but that you recognize that the past has given birth to a future. Church anniversaries should no longer memorialize the past, but emphasize the new mission ventures of the future.

2) Use only "proscriptive" mandates

Complete the process of rewriting all job descriptions and mandates proscriptively. This includes rewriting job descriptions for support staff such as custodians and secretaries.

3) Rely on PALS processes

Eliminate any remaining committees, so that all work is done by teams based on the faith-building and relationship-building processes of the PALS strategy. In place of annual evaluations, initiate quarterly opportunities to upgrade skills and verify boundaries.

4) Confirm the visionary board

Discard any remaining vestiges of board management, and confirm board members' roles as spiritual leaders who model the core values and beliefs of the congregation and look far into the future. Refer to pages 41-61 and 124-25 of *Christian Chaos* for a description of the visionary board.

5) Confirm the stability triangle

Discard any remaining vestiges of hierarchy, and confirm the three teams of the stability triangle to do whatever is necessary to grow, train, and deploy leaders. Refer to pages 77-93 and 126-27 of *Christian Chaos* for a full description of the stability triangle.

6) Identify trusteeship

Make whatever legal or polity adjustments are necessary to reassign trusteeship to the administration team. Publicly articulate the role of trusteeship to be one of resourcing mission, rather than maintaining assets.

7) Routinely discern gifts

Establish a monthly pattern for gifts discernment and coaching that is open to people within and beyond the church. Combine gifts discernment with personality inventories, or any other method for personal, relational, and spiritual growth.

8) "Rear load" adult education

Make sure that there are clearly articulated, high expectations for adult spiritual growth, but that these come only *after* newcomers have easily and completely accessed the worship life of the church and experienced change through the touch of the Holy.

9) Multitrack worship

Develop multiple options for worship in style and mission purpose, and target specific publics in the community for indigenous worship. Make sure a team of volunteers guides each track of worship.

10) Confirm coaching/training role of staff

Avoid hiring professionals to do ministry, and concentrate on growing future church leaders from within the congregation. Anticipate future hiring to be linked to specific mission expertise.

11) Fine-tune pastoral relations

Assess whether or not current staff completely own and articulate the congregational consensus around core values, beliefs, vision, and mission. Insist in judicatory interaction that newly appointed or called clergy accept the nontraditional roles of leadership now in place, and celebrate the congregational identity.

139

12) Focus continuing education for clergy

Discern the new skills that clergy must learn, and provide funding, freedom, and personal support for clergy (or clergy families or both) to go wherever, and consult with whomever, in order to obtain new skills.

13) Routinely grow cell-group leaders

Establish a routine to identify and train laity to become the effective "pastors" of small groups in the church. Insofar as state and provincial laws permit, equip cell-group leaders to do the "life cycle ministries" once associated with clergy, so that clergy are empowered to baptize, consecrate marriages, and lead funeral services.

14) Routinely count the whole cost of discipleship

Routinely consider the costs of discipleship in the context of any new initiative or creative idea, and plan to meet the cost of changing heritage, attitude, leadership, and organization *before* worrying about meeting costs for property and finance. Develop a clear, simple, transparent grievance process similar to the outline in *Christian Chaos* (pages 132-39).

15) Create new budgeting and stewardship processes

Orient the budget entirely to mission, and create as many options as possible for teams to raise funds. The new stewardship posture is, "How can we help you raise the money you need for your mission?" Develop capital pools to seed emerging mission. Empower mission teams to manage their own funds.

16) Multitrack giving

Multiply options to give to specific ministries using diverse financial vehicles for preauthorized withdrawals, credit, debit, cash machine, bequest, and so on.

17) Follow faith with beneficial service

Insist that evangelism be linked to social change, so that no mission team ever shares faith without simultaneously doing something to benefit the world.

18) Communicate faith motivations for social service

Insist that social action be linked to evangelism, so that no bene-

140

ficial service is ever done without simultaneously articulating the faith motivation that lies behind it.

19) Renovate, relocate, and upgrade

Do whatever is necessary to change property or upgrade technology to better communicate the gospel to the multiple publics in the community. For a deeper insight into property and technology change, see *Coaching Change*.

20) Tell the stories of personal and social transformation

Aggressively market the stories of positive and personal change locally, regionally, and globally, so that the public recognizes the congregation immediately, and associates the congregation with a particular vision apart from its denominational affiliation.

Stress   *Kicking Habits* identifies the stress you can expect during this fifth stage of transformation. Read pages 231-34 once again. Experience from those who have used *Kicking Habits* as a guide to change reveals that the stress here is what one might expect from perceptive, recovering addicts who know that they cannot rest, but must continue the self-discipline that celebrates the intervention of a Higher Power and walk one day at a time with Jesus into the twenty-first century.

1) The constant financial challenge

The vision of the thriving church always outdistances its financial reserves. Churches do not rely on invested capital reserves for financial security, but on the skill and ability of their financial leaders. Sound debt management is the key to their success. Thriving churches are probably more aggressive and open about money than declining churches, but for different reasons. Declining churches are desperate for money in order to stay alive. Thriving churches are desperate for money in order to advance the realm of God one more step.

Church leaders need to be ever more careful about the spiritual integrity of their financial leaders, and about the fiscal responsibility of their pastoral leaders. The advice and coaching they receive is more likely going to come from business, nonprofit, and parachurch colleagues, rather than from traditional denominational sources.

2) The constant learning curve

The mission opportunities of the thriving church always outdistance the particular skills that the leaders have at any given time. Their church leaders are constantly learning, changing, experimenting, and growing. The constant feeling of inadequacy will be a positive motivation only if the church forgives mistakes, rewards experiments, and supports continuing education.

Thriving churches need to dramatically increase continuing education budgets for clergy and laity, and allow leaders the freedom to go anywhere and learn from anyone. The training they receive is more likely going to be obtained from global mission partners, other professional disciplines, other thriving congregations beyond the judicatory, or nontraditional educational institutions, rather than from traditional seminaries.

3) The constant imbalance between leaders and newcomers

The number of newcomers in thriving churches always outdistances the number of gifted, called, and equipped leaders churches deploy. They never have enough cell-group leaders, mission-team leaders, worship leaders, or staff. Although this may seem like a nice problem to have, there is constant risk that newcomers will not receive the spiritual guidance and coaching they need in a timely way. Their discouragement can rapidly cause the growth of the church to plateau.

Thriving churches cannot allow themselves to be distracted by single issues, denominational demands, or irrelevant disputes that will take energy away from growing Christians to become leaders in their own right. This requires a single-mindedness that is fanatical about volunteer empowerment, but not about any particular issue or program. A church's staff and volunteer leaders will become extremely impatient with irrelevant bureaucracy, attempts to arbitrarily relocate clergy, or pointless denominational meetings.

4) The constant critique of success

Thriving churches always suffer more from success than they do from failure. Their discipline to learn from mistakes allows them to overcome failure. Their success, however, invites the jealous condemnation of other community churches and their denominational parents. Oddly enough, their very success forces them to always prove their faithfulness! Declining churches that are dying are rarely accused of being unfaithful, even though their accommodation to the culture of the eighteenth and nineteenth centuries has literally poisoned their ability to adapt to the twenty-first century. Thriving churches are accused of cultural accommodation, even though their leaders spend more time motivating spiritual growth and reflecting on mission integrity than anyone else.

Thriving churches are motivated to become teaching centers partly out of a sense of mission to transform the church, and partly out of self-interest. If their critics just spend time with the congregation, and engage their congregational leaders in a dialogue between equals, the force of their criticisms disappears.

Transformation never ends, and neither does the stress of transformation. Once the three to seven years of anticipated stress are over, transformational leaders become gleefully aware that the process of constant, revolutionary change has only just begun.

In *Kicking Habits,* the contrast between the declining church system and the thriving church system is described as the difference between a system that is "all about belonging" and a system that is "all about changing." Usually, that difference implies that the declining church is preoccupied with assimilating new institutional members, while the thriving church is preoccupied with transforming individual lives. However, the system that is "all about change" is much more than that. The very organization is in constant flux. If one were to go away for a year or two, and return to the church, it would no longer be the same. The very church organization itself is in constant change. You might return to discover that—

the staff configuration is different;
the sanctuary has been completely renovated;
the church is located twelve blocks away;
the principle language spoken is no longer English.

These or any number of other changes may have occurred. All you have to do is blink, and this church has experienced another revolution.

Yet it all happens with joy, hope, and confidence that in the end makes the spiritual entrepreneur feel once again right at home.

WHAT DO WE DO NOW?

Your study of *Kicking Habits* (Upgrade Edition) has now taken twenty or more sessions to complete, or about a quarter of the year.

- Perhaps you have been studying the book from September through the early days of Advent.
- Perhaps you have been studying from January to the early days of Easter.
- Perhaps you began studying during Lent, and have now come to Pentecost.

I hope that you have begun to have a sense of urgency, and found a deeper hope for your church. You have several options.

Option #1: If you would rather die with dignity than change, remain faithful to Christ by planning now to disperse the assets of your church (property and financial investments) to assist fledgling new congregations thrive in life and mission elsewhere in your community or the world. You may do this by consulting with your denominational judicatory leaders, or on your own. Do it. Please write a "will" so that others will live.

Option #2: If you would rather change than die, obtain my book *Facing Reality: A Congregational Mission Assessment Tool* and do the hard work and research necessary to maximize your strengths, address your weaknesses, and heal the hidden patterns of corporate addiction that block your best intentions. Do it now, do it together, and do *not* delegate it to an ad hoc committee! Since you have finished this study guide, you have already begun to answer many of the questions in the *Congregational Mission Assessment.*

Option #3:   If you tend to think in linear ways, and love strategic planning, follow the five stages outlined in *Kicking Habits* and explained tactically here in *Coming Clean.* Start with stage 1, and keep working until the end. Just remember you don't have to do it all tomorrow, just take little steps and never look back!

Option #4:   If you tend to think in lateral ways, and love chaos and entrepreneurship, then read the "Ministry Mapping" section (pages 239-78) in my book *Moving Off the Map*, and practice coaching and leveraging change using the leverage points I describe in *Coaching Change: Breaking Down Resistance, Building Up Hope.*

There are other options, of course. There are many other tools and resources for transformation. Choose what works for you. The best resources are from independent sources, rather than denominational sources. The best process relies on congregational leadership, rather than denominational leadership. However, the best way to succeed is to ask your denomination to pray for you, resource you with training funds, and network you with other like-hearted congregations nearby and around the world. Take initiative now! Do it in networks and partnerships! And remember, Jesus is with you always, even to the end of the age!

LEADING CHANGE

A Bible Study for Those Who Want to Be
Transformational Leaders

1 CORINTHIANS 13

In the context of corporate addiction, transformational leadership has sometimes been compared to tough love amid dysfunctional families. There is merit in the comparison. Transformational leaders show no mercy when it comes to helping the church regain its authentic spiritual health and vitality. However, there are more dimensions to tough love than many transformational leaders realize. You are in a dynamic, synergistic relationship. Those who would transform a congregation must be prepared to be transformed themselves.

Transformation will be tough on you. It is not just that resistant controllers can abuse, hurt, or slander you and those you love. There will be constant self-doubts, unpredictable and incredibly stupid mistakes, perpetual feelings of inadequacy, anxiety for the strain on your family life, and the never-ending battle to curb your impatience. Here are some of the remarks transformation leaders usually make when they reflect on their experience.

> *"I never really knew what I was getting myself into!"*
> *"If I could do it all over again, there is a lot I would do differently!"*
> *"I should have paid more attention to my own mental, relational, and spiritual well-being!"*
> *"I am a better person, and a very different leader, than I thought I would be!"*
> *"I'm not sure who changed more: the congregation, the mission field, or me!"*

Leaders who express tough love for their congregations must expect

God to express tough love toward them. Transformation is a glorious adventure, and the ultimate experience of a thriving church is a tremendous joy for all. Yet there is a cost to such discipleship. You yourself will have to grow beyond anger, frustration, fear, and judgment of self or others to a more perfect state of love. Of all the gifts to be discerned, that is the most precious and the most difficult of all.

I offer the following paraphrase of 1 Corinthians 13 for your private meditation. It is presented in three parts. I urge you to read one part at a time, pray in silence, and discuss in gentle honesty.

The Challenge

If I speak in the tongues of mortals and angels,
    If I speak the language of every public in the community,
    And if I can communicate in every media,
But do not have love,
I am a noisy nuisance or a clanging controller.

And if I have prophetic powers,
    And understand all the mysteries of church growth
    And possess every postmodern skill,
    And if I possess all faith, so as to remove the most daunting
      obstacles of capital funding,
But do not have love,
I am nothing but a dreamer, a theorist, a technician, and a fund-raiser.

If I give away all my possessions,
    even to the sacrifice of the parsonage and the pension plan,
    and even if I hand over my body to be burned by the personnel
      committee and the board,
    so that I may boast of my single-minded commitment,
But do not have love,
I gain nothing but broken health, broken family life, and broken
    dreams.

The Life

Love is patient; love is kind;
    Love repeats itself over, and over, and over again until, one day,
      a sleeper awakes;

148

Love holds the fragile, newborn mission child of every Christian in
tender arms.

Love is not envious, or boastful, or arrogant, or rude.

Love does not try to duplicate the megachurch next door,

or gleefully brag about numerical growth or capital gains,

or cluck dismissively over the failings of their denominational
colleagues,

or demean the integrity of veteran church members, no matter
what century they appear to be living in.

It does not insist on its own way,

but only that, whatever the way, it be with Jesus;

It is not irritable or resentful,

but restless and resourceful.

It does not rejoice in wrongdoing, but rejoices in the truth.

It overturns the tables of controlling self-interest,

And cracks the whip on the status quo,

And disempowers the intimidators of the least of Christ's
brothers and sisters;

Because the truth is the only gospel that matters and nothing else,

And the truth is that hierarchy and bureaucracy don't work
anymore,

And the truth is that the meek shall inherit the earth.

It bears all things,

Even the insults, slanders, telephone campaigns, and anonymous
reports to the bishop that "many people are angry and threat-
ening to leave the church";

It believes all things,

Even that light is more powerful than darkness,

and that grace will be sufficient;

It hopes all things,

Even that the slowest clergy and laity will finally "get it,"

and that the breakthrough into thriving church life will eventually come,

and that the Gentiles will indeed experience Christ, in a whole
new way, and be set free.

It endures all things,

Even the interminable mystery of not knowing what will happen
next,

and the discovery that what does happen is not exactly what
you have prepared for.

149

The Hope

Love never ends.
    The relationship with Christ just goes on, and on, and on,
    and the intimacy with others goes deeper, and deeper, and deeper,
    and the self-esteem and serenity grows richer, and richer, and richer.
As for prophecies, they will come to an end,
    and the strategy that works well today will be inadequate for
        tomorrow.
As for tongues, they will cease,
    and the critics of today will eventually weary, move on, or die.
As for knowledge, it will come to an end,
    and God's wisdom will begin when and where I myself am at my
        wit's end.
For we know only in part,
and we prophesy only in part,
But when the complete comes, the partial will come to an end,
    And then even I will finally "get it,"
    And then the breakthrough into abundant life will eventually
        come to me,
    And then my family and I will experience Christ, in a whole new
        way, and be set free.

The Bottom Line

When I was a child,
I spoke like a child,
    And said things I didn't quite mean, and meant things I didn't
        quite understand.
I thought like a child,
    And imagined fears that never came, and realized joys without
        knowing their true value.
I reasoned like a child,
    And deduced dogmas rather than questions, and questioned what
        was obviously true.
When I became an adult, I put an end to childish ways.
For now we see in a mirror, dimly,
    And the face of the transforming congregation is the face of my
        transforming self,
But then we will see face-to-face,

And to see the face of even my worst enemy will be like seeing
  the face of God.
Now I know only in part,
  And the future of our community of disciples is unclear even to
  me.
Then I will know fully,
  And the fullness of our mission will be treasured by the public
  and beloved by God,
Even as I myself have been fully known,
  And my weakness and my strength shall be acceptable to Christ.

And now faith, hope, and love abide, these three;
  Faith in the transforming power of God,
  Hope in the fulfillment of the Spirit,
  Love for Christ, and Christ alone.
And the greatest of these is love.

No transformation will happen for your church unless a leader guides it. These leaders do not need to have all the answers, or possess all the tactical skills. However, these leaders do need to be willing to risk the transformation of their own lives, right along with the transformation of their church.

1. The leaders of transformation are not caregivers, but unmercifully honest. If you really love people inside the church, you must help them face their addictions.

2. The leaders of transformation are not strategic planners, but imaginatively intuitive. If you really love people outside the church, you must seize the moment for timely intervention.

3. The leaders of transformation are not heritage protectors, but breathtakingly daring. If you really love Jesus, you do whatever it takes to share the gospel.

It really is all about love. Church leaders are like Simon Peter at breakfast on the Sea of Galilee. We are frying all the favorite fish that for centuries were the staples of our spiritual diet. And Jesus says, "Simon son of John, do you love me more than these?"

INDEX

addiction, 25, 85, 88-89, 120
administration, 76
Administration Team, 77, 129
affinity group, 72
annual meeting, 130
attitude, 86, 119

baptism, 15
board, 116, 129, 138
budget, 54, 119, 140

calling, 53-56
caregiving, 120
change, 143
chaos, 114
children, 49
Christ focus, 43
church growth, 39
clergy roles, 17
coaching, 56
codependency, 120
communication, 110, 130
conflict, 53, 56
consensus, 132
control, 56, 111, 121
core process, 40
counseling, 118

denomination, 53
diversity, 67
drama, 108

ecstasy, 109
education, 46, 99, 139, 142
egotism, 50
energy field, 66-70, 121, 125-27, 133, 138

failure, 52
finance, 116, 129-30, 141
fruits of Spirit, 67
fulfillment, 50

gaps, 136
genetic code, 125, 133, 138
gifts, 47, 97, 100, 120, 139
good worship, 44

Human Resources Team, 77, 128

inadequacy, 112
inclusivity, 67
intimacy, 109

key question, 100

lay counselors, 108
lay leaders, 118, 128, 140
leadership, 113, 119
lectionary, 108

mandates, 116, 130
mapping, 135
material things, 57
membership, 47, 71, 107
mentor, 119
ministry, 51
mission, 51, 74-75, 83, 97, 136
model, 70
music, 81, 108, 111
myths of modernity, 104

name, 131
nominations, 97

open space, 109
organization, 76, 97, 122-34

partnerships, 119
personal growth, 46-49, 73, 121, 125
personnel support, 139
policy, 116
preaching, 95
procedure, 95
process, 10

redundancy, 137

skills, 112, 117
small groups, 72, 131
spiritual growth, 102, 103, 121, 125, 136
stability triangle, 75, 139
staff, 55, 70, 98, 139
stewardship, 129, 140
strategic planning, 51, 85-86
stress, 9, 11
system, 39

team, 58, 97, 119, 126, 130, 141
touch of the Holy, 43
training, 99, 117
training team, 77, 131
triads, 110, 122

Uncontrollable Holy, 111
urgency, 42, 58, 103

values, 67-70
vision, 67-70, 93, 100
visitation, 117

worship, 44, 80, 104-12, 139
worship teams, 109

yearning, 38, 73
youth, 49

SCRIPTURES

Nehemiah 8:9-10 63

Mark 5:1-20 25

Luke 5:17-26 42
Luke 9:60 86
Luke 10 86
Luke 19:1-11 35
Luke 24:13-32 46

John 11:1-44 90
John 12:9-11 90

Acts 2:1-17, 36-47 40
Acts 2:43-47; 4:32-35; 6:1-4 . . .75
Acts 10:1-12 57
Acts 13:1-3 57
Acts 15:1-11, 19-21 66
Acts 16 . . . . .80, 87
Acts 18:1-3, 18, 24-28 50

Romans 16:1-16 71

1 Corinthians 1:18-25 67
1 Corinthians 1:26-31 50
1 Corinthians 3:1-15,
   21-23 124
1 Corinthians 13 147

Galatians 5:22-26 67

Philippians 3:7-16 135
Philippians 4:4-9 80

James 1:19-25; 2:14-17 54

Revelation 1:1-8; 21:1-7;
   22:1-5 92
Revelation 3:14-22 103
Revelation 27:1-44 113

PRAYER FOCI

perpetual motion 25
video shopping mall 34
old photos 42
empty frame 46
time of crisis 48
membership expectation . . .48
seven acts of mercy 50
motivational slogans 53
planet earth 57
magnetic coil 66

lava lamp 71
stool and dishes 75
worship video 80
strobe light 92
film of birth 102
Poseidon Adventure clip . . .113
potted plant 123
soda pop 134
balloon burst 134

EXERCISES

stress test 27-34

spiritual yearning 38

croquet and jai alai 41

key question 44

worship expectations 44

creative ideas 52

social service 55

pastor's energies 56

worship newcomers 58

teams or task groups 59

tornado 61-62

tidal wave 64-65

T-shirts 68

market survey 70

personal growth 74

mission checklist 78

stool and dishes 79

worship benefits 82

myths of modernity 104